TOMB KINGS
By Robin Cruddace

CONTENTS

Art: John Blanche, Alex Boyd, Kevin Chin, Paul Dainton, Dave Gallagher, Neil Hodgson, Nuala Kinrade, Adrian Smith. **Book Design:** Carl Dafforn, Emma Parrington, Mark Raynor. **'Eavy Metal:** Neil Green, David Heathfield, Mark Holmes, Kornel Kozak, Darren Latham, Keith Robertson, Joe Tomaszewski, Anja Wettergren. **Games Development:** Robin Cruddace, Matthew Hobday, Jervis Johnson, Phil Kelly, Mark Latham, Jeremy Vetock, Sarah Wallen, Matthew Ward. **Hobby Team:** Dave Andrews, Nick Bayton, Mark Jones, Chad Mierzwa, Chris Peach, Duncan Rhodes. **Miniatures Design:** Mike Anderson, Giorgio Bassani, Trish Carden, Juan Diaz, Martin Footitt, Mike Fores, Jes Goodwin, Colin Grayson, Mark Harrison, Alex Hedström, Matt Holland, Neil Langdown, Aly Morrison, Brian Nelson, Oliver Norman, Seb Perbet, Alan Perry, Michael Perry, Dale Stringer, Dave Thomas, Tom Walton. **Photography:** Glenn More. **Production & Reprographics:** Simon Burton, Chris Eggar, Marc Elliott, Zaff Haydn-Davies, Kris Jaggers, John Michelbach, Melissa Roberts, Rachel Ryan, James Shardlow, Kris Shield, Markus Trenkner. **Previous Editions:** Alessio Cavatore, Jervis Johnson, Bill King, Graham McNeill, Space McQuirk, Anthony Reynolds, Gav Thorpe. **Special Thanks to:** Stu Black, Ben Curry, Adam Hall, Ben Johnson, Andrew Kenrick, Alan Merrett, Rick Priestley, Chris Taylor.

UK
Games Workshop Ltd.,
Willow Rd, Lenton,
Nottingham.
NG7 2WS

Northern Europe
Games Workshop Ltd,
Willow Rd, Lenton,
Nottingham.
NG7 2WS, UK

North America
Games Workshop Inc,
6211 East Holmes Road,
Memphis.
Tennessee 38141

Australia
Games Workshop,
23 Liverpool Street,
Ingleburn.
NSW 2565

www.games-workshop.com

INTRODUCTION

Welcome to *Warhammer: Tomb Kings*, your indispensable guide to the ancient and wrathful denizens of the cursed Land of the Dead. This book provides all the information you'll require to collect and play with a Tomb Kings army in games of Warhammer.

WHY COLLECT TOMB KINGS?

The Tomb Kings are the true monarchs of the Undead. They ruled a vast and mighty civilisation at a time when other men were still barbarians, and now, thousands of years after their deaths, they have been awakened. Rising from their sarcophagi, the mummified Tomb Kings possess the same thirst for conquest that drove them in life. They are coming to reclaim their rightful dominion over the kingdoms of the living, and woe betide any that stand in their way.

A Tomb Kings army arrayed on the battlefield is a spectacular sight to behold. The undead legions comprise rank upon rank of skeletal soldiers – great phalanxes of gleaming bone decorated with bronze and gold – regiments of Undead cavalry and gilded chariots, mummified heroes and immortal kings, and towering war-statues carved in the images of mythical monsters and ancient gods. The Tomb Kings are a merciless and implacable force, one that will not stop until its foes have been utterly crushed.

HOW THIS BOOK WORKS

Warhammer Armies books are split into sections, each of which deals with a different aspect of the army. *Warhammer: Tomb Kings* contains:

- **Kings of the Dead.** This section describes the history of the Tomb Kings, including the rise of Nehekhara, its kings' obsession with mortality, and the treachery that cursed the entire realm to undeath. Also included is a map of the Land of the Dead and descriptions of the many bloody conquests fought as the Tomb Kings and their legions battled to restore majesty to their former kingdoms.

- **The Legions of the Tomb Kings.** Each and every troop type in the Tomb Kings army is examined here. You will find a full description of each unit, alongside complete rules of any special abilities or options they possess. This section also details the spells of the arcane Lore of Nehekhara and the Treasures of the Necropolis – magical artefacts that are unique to the Tomb Kings – along with rules to use them in your games.

- **The Dead Awaken.** Here you will find a showcase of the range of Citadel miniatures available for the Tomb Kings army, gloriously painted by Games Workshop's world-renowned 'Eavy Metal team.

- **Tomb Kings Army List.** The army list takes all of the characters, warriors, monsters and war machines presented in the Legions of the Tomb Kings section, and arranges them so you can choose an army for your games. Units are classed as characters (Lord or Heroes), Core, Special or Rare, and can be taken in different quantities depending on the size of the game you are playing.

FIND OUT MORE

While *Warhammer: Tomb Kings* contains everything you need to play a game with your army, there are always more tactics to use, different battles to fight and new painting ideas to try out. The monthly magazine *White Dwarf* contains articles about all aspects of the Warhammer hobby, and you can find articles specific to the Tomb Kings on our website:

www.games-workshop.com

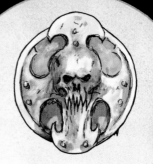

KINGS OF THE DEAD

Across the arid deserts of Nehekhara, vast legions of skeletal soldiers rise up from beneath the baking sands to slaughter those that trespass into their domain. It is a lifeless realm with endless dunes stained red with the blood of savages and barbarians. This is the Land of the Dead, where mummified kings are cursed to rule in perpetual unlife. But it was not always thus.

There once was a time when the ancient kingdom of Nehekhara stood as the crown of human civilisation; a golden age when its cities shone with majestic splendour, its armies conquered entire nations and its kings ruled as gods amongst men. But this great realm was razed millennia ago through treachery and sorcery; the living perished in an instant, and the dead rose from their tombs. This is the tale of those times...

THE TOMB KINGS

Far to the south of the Old World lies a desolate, wind-swept desert. No living thing stirs in this place, but it is far from uninhabited. This is Nehekhara, the cursed Land of the Dead, and the domain of the Tomb Kings.

Nehekhara was once a land of magnificent architecture and noble dynasties. Its warrior kings led golden armies against the barbarian tribes that envied the splendour of Nehekhara, and the greenskin hordes that constantly threatened their realm. They fought their wars with phalanxes of spearmen that stretched across battlefields as far as the eye could see, with regiments of archers that darkened the skies with arrows and with battalions of deadly chariots that rumbled across the land. The Nehekharans crushed all before them in displays of martial brilliance until their realm reached from the lizard-infested Southlands to the monster-haunted forests of the north. However, the vain kings refused to let mere death cheat them of their lifetime's accomplishments or rob them of their worldly possessions. It was the belief of every Nehekharan king that, upon his death, he would be mummified in an elaborate ceremony and interred within a magnificent burial pyramid. Here they would await the Day of Awakening, when they would arise into a golden paradise filled with all their subjects and belongings, which were necessarily entombed alongside their lords, and here would they reign supreme for all eternity. Over time, their necropolises became bigger and grander than the towns of the living. It is said that the honoured dead buried beneath Nehekhara outnumber those that breathe in the Old World twice over, and the dead do not rest easy…

RULERS OF THE DEAD

Through blasphemous necromantic magic, the entire population of Nehekhara was cursed to a living death. The corrupt sorcerer Nagash instigated a great catastrophe that at once destroyed every living thing in Nehekhara, and raised the dead from their tombs. The Tomb Kings arose from their sleep of oblivion prematurely, albeit immortal and more powerful than ever. The once-proud rulers of Nehekhara have been reborn into a mocking travesty of life. They have awoken from the slumber of death to discover that they are repulsive Undead creatures; bone-dry cadavers whose once palatial realms are but a shadow of their former splendour. They found Nehekhara plagued by hordes of barbaric invaders; its ancient cities and proud statuary crumbling from long centuries of warfare and its bountiful riches plundered by countless tomb robbers. The Tomb Kings now fight to restore their vast empire to its former majesty, striking forth from the desert to reclaim the world from the living.

The Tomb Kings' trusted advisors were their Liche Priests – wizards of great power whose sole task in life was to prepare the kings' tombs and ensure their lasting immortality. When a king died, his Liche Priests would embalm his body in an elaborate funeral ceremony and inter his remains in preparation for the Day of Awakening. The undying Liche Priests, withered and frail from the passing of untold centuries, are now responsible for watching over Nehekhara and for reawakening the armies of the Tomb Kings to glorious conquest.

THE CURSE OF UNDEATH

The Tomb Kings reign from their necropolises as they have always done, imitating the life they once knew. Many Tomb Kings behave as if nothing were awry, ruling as if they were still beings of flesh and blood. Perhaps some are truly unaware that they are Undead, whilst others are in denial of their cursed existence or have been driven mad by the sight of their own hideous visage. A Tomb King may demand a bowl of sweet figs and a goblet of fine wine, seemingly oblivious that the contents of such a meal would spill through their desiccated bodies onto the floor. When the proffered meal arrives, a Tomb King will simply stare at the fruit, wondering what such a thing is for, until it either rots to dust or a vestigial memory surfaces allowing a moment of clarity to reassert itself. In that instant, the Tomb King recalls all the pride, majesty and greatness of what he was and the cruel parody of what he has become. Realising that he will never know the taste of food, the quenching relief of cool water, the sensation of touch or any other simple joy ever again, the Tomb King will enter a fit of incandescent rage. Ancient and wrathful, all that is left for the Tomb Kings is their hunger for power, their thirst for conquest and their need for vengeance. The Tomb Kings are unremitting in their eternal war upon those who have the temerity to live whilst their rightful rulers languish in undeath.

THE UNDYING LEGIONS

In ancient Nehekhara, a ruler was only as powerful as his force under arms. Thus, the kings maintained vast legions and proclaimed their victories proudly so that rivals would know of their strength and tremble. In this way, the names of many legions became legendary. King Nekhesh's Scorpion Legion, for example, halted several barbarian invasions and felled their foes with spears whose tips were fashioned from the black claws of giant scorpions. Similarly, Prince Sekhef's Heralds of Death were feared for their grisly standard, from which the skulls of a dozen conquered kings hung, cursed by the Liche Priests of Numas to wail in perpetual torment. These and a thousand others have now awakened from death, striking fear into the hearts of their enemies once more.

It was the duty of every soldier to serve his king, not only in life but beyond into death. Countless thousands of loyal warriors were buried alive in the great tomb pits of the ancient kings. Assembled in serried ranks as though on parade, the legions of each king were entombed with all the weapons and regalia of war needed to protect their lord in the next life – bronze-tipped spears, curved swords and

sturdy shields. Many archers were also buried with their masters, together with huge stockpiles of magically blessed arrows. Alongside the foot soldiery of the king's legions were regiments of cavalry and gilded chariots, which awaited the day when they would gallop out of the mortuary-pyramids and crush their enemies once again.

When the Tomb Kings advance to war, they do so with these vast legions at their command, a breathtaking sight of gleaming bone, gold and bronze. The Undead warriors stride unfalteringly across the searing desert and through howling sandstorms as they close in on their foes. Vast phalanxes of skeletal soldiers advance towards their terrified enemies in relentless unison, fighting with a supernatural discipline that no mortal man can hope to match. Slowly but implacably, the legions of the Undead drive their foes before them, guided as always by the unyielding will of their Tomb King.

There are some necromantic spells that reanimate long-dead corpses, creating Undead automatons that serve the necromancer in a mindless fashion. Such is not the way of the Tomb Kings' soldiers; each Skeleton in the numberless legions is inhabited by the soul of an ancient Nehekharan warrior. Through the magical incantations of Liche Priests, spirits of loyal soldiers are summoned from the Realm of Souls and bound within corporeal remains. These warriors are not, then, slaves to the will of an evil wizard, but dutiful soldiers who unswervingly obey their king's commands in death, just as they once had in life. However, without the extensive mummification techniques and magical wards of preservation laid upon the bodies of the Nehekharan royalty, the Skeletons of the Tomb Kings' legions perceive the world very differently to mortal men. They retain only the most pertinent aspects of their former lives: the endless years of training and discipline, the martial skills honed on countless fields of battle and, above all else, their oaths of fealty to their king. Personality and ambition are ephemeral, and even their names have faded like half-forgotten dreams.

THE TOWERING STATUES

To protect the corpses of the kings throughout eternity, the ancient Nehekharans wrought magnificent statues to guard over their royal tombs. These towering sculptures, made in the images of gods, kings and mythical creatures, were placed in and around the necropolises. Titanic warriors hewn from cliff-faces and giant beasts built from whitest marble, darkest obsidian and blood-forged gold stood sentry beside every entranceway. Ranks of imposing Ushabti – statuary carved in the images of a pantheon of ancient gods – lined the labyrinthine corridors of the burial pyramids.

"And behold, the almighty god-king Settra did awaken from his sleep of blessed oblivion. His legions, long buried beneath the sands, did arise and stand to attention, awaiting his order. And he did say 'War', and the world did tremble..."

– *Grand Hierophant Khatep*

Monstrous sphinxes loomed over the sacred sarcophagi of the Tomb Kings themselves and countless other, more terrifying statues, lay buried and forgotten beneath the baking sands.

The Liche Priests learned long ago that the same incantations used to summon forth warrior-spirits could be adapted to animate the hulking stone forms of Nehekhara's fearsome statuary. Ever since, when the Tomb Kings have made war upon their enemies, constructs of animated stone have fought beside them. These imposing figures wade through the ranks of mortals, crushing their opponents with terrible blows as enemy arrows and sword-strokes rebound harmlessly from their rock-hard frames.

RE-CONQUEST OF AN EMPIRE

The reborn Tomb Kings look upon their shattered lands and skeletal legions, and they are greatly angered. Nehekhara was once a powerful and proud nation, and its enemies cowered before the might of its kings and the strength of its armies. Year upon year its borders expanded, and with the conquered wealth magnificent monuments were raised to honour kings and gods. The Tomb Kings have vowed that all of Nehekhara must be restored. They will not stop until every city is rebuilt, every land re-conquered and every stolen treasure, even the most insignificant of trinkets, is recovered.

So as it once was, so will it be again.

THE RISE OF SETTRA

The ancient kingdom of Nehekhara was at its most powerful when other men were still primitive and savage – about two and a half millennia before the coming of the barbarian hero Sigmar Heldenhammer.

Through centuries of work and culture, Nehekhara, known to its people as the Great Land, was built into a powerful civilisation. Its people built great cities out of white stone and carved marble. They constructed vast roads and fleets of ships to connect each city to its neighbours. Mighty kings, whose every whim was law, ruled the people. Vast armies of disciplined soldiers were raised and trained in the king's name, and those that invaded their cities were mercilessly cut down. Greatest of these cities was Khemri – the City of Kings – and by tradition, whoever ruled there was considered first amongst equals. The other cities were each governed by their own king, though all were expected to show loyalty and pay tribute to Khemri. Together, these kings subdued the tribes in the surrounding lands, drove back the greenskin hordes that plagued the realm, and ruled from the western Deserts of Araby to the eastern Sea of Dread. At the height of Nehekhara's power, it had expanded and conquered lands as far north as what is now laughably called the Empire, south into the primordial jungles of the Southlands and even east into the foreboding Dark Lands. The kings' armies marched across the world subjugating all before them, and their vast fleets of galleys and war barques terrorised the Great Ocean.

THE TIME BEFORE MAN

According to the myths and legends of Nehekhara, in the times before men, gods walked the world as mortals. It was believed by the ancient Nehekharans that when the Desert Gods first arrived in the Great Land, they fought the armies of vile Daemons and foul spirits that lurked there in great battles that lasted for many centuries. In numerous inscriptions, carved on the tombs and monuments of ancient cities, it is written that Ptra, the Sun God and King of the Nehekharan pantheon, led the final battle against the dark powers. Riding a resplendent golden chariot, he drove the darkness back; even the most powerful Daemon recoiled from the touch of his divine light. Ptra and the Desert Gods were victorious, and the evil ones retreated north to escape destruction.

Legend says that the Desert Gods then transformed the lands into a verdant realm and ruled there for thousands of years until the birth of the race of Man. It is said that these people were so favoured by the heavens that Ptra himself bestowed upon them the fertile land that would later be called Nehekhara. In exchange for their worship, the deities offered to protect and watch over those that dwelt in the Great Land. With the covenant made, the gods nurtured the people of the nomadic tribes, teaching them how to read, write and build great cities. Thus was the Nehekharan civilisation born.

STRIFE IN THE GREAT LAND

Though Nehekhara prospered and its cities grew in size, wealth and influence, the kings thirsted for ever greater power. To this end they began to war upon each other. Over the following years, the Crown of Nehekhara, a symbol of rulership over all of the Great Land, passed from king to conquering king. Dozens of kings rose and fell during this time, so many that their names are not remembered, but it is known that none had the strength to prevail or maintain power for long.

With every Nehekharan city's military might turned upon its neighbours, the Great Land was open to attack from invaders. The city of Lybaras was almost completely destroyed by the scaled creatures that lurked within the southern jungles. Numerous greenskin hordes and barbarous tribes of men descended from the north, destroying and slaughtering as they rampaged unchecked across Nehekhara. During this time the Great Land was also stricken with drought and plague. No single city's army, exhausted as they were from disease, starvation and unremitting civil war, could hope to hold back the tide alone, but the arrogant and distrustful kings refused to put aside their differences to form a lasting alliance, bow their knee to another or halt in their pursuit of domination over their rivals. The first great civilisation of Man stood on the brink of destruction. Unless the Nehekharans could be unified, they would all perish.

SETTRA THE GREAT

The Nehekharan priesthood saw the strife in the Great Land as a sign that the gods were angered, but their warnings and protestations to the warring kings fell on deaf ears. That all changed with the coming of Settra.

Of all the kings of Nehekhara, none could match the splendour, cruelty and arrogance of Settra, the newly crowned king of Khemri. He was a vain and egotistical man, and demanded not only the obedience, but also the adoration of his subjects. However, Settra was no fool, and when he listened to his priests he realised that only a leader who could command the respect of the gods would earn the full adulation of the people. To this end, Settra, alone amongst all the kings of Nehekhara, paid homage to the ancient gods; early in his reign he ordered the restoration of temples and erected many magnificent statues to be built in their honour.

On the first anniversary of his coronation, Settra beseeched the gods to restore Khemri to its former glory and grant him the strength to conquer his rivals, sacrificing his own children in a grand ritual to show his commitment and prove his worth. The next day, the Great Vitae River flooded for the first time in several decades. With the waters, disease was washed away from Khemri and the crop harvest was plentiful for the first time in living memory. This was seen as a sign by both the Nehekharan priesthood and the populace of Khemri that Settra was indeed chosen by the gods. So it was that Settra became the first Priest King of Khemri, a ruler who commanded not only the unswerving loyalty of his people and his legions, but who also wielded the power of the gods.

Settra was a powerful king who had fought alongside his father's legions for many years before ascending to Khemri's throne. He was a ruthless warlord, and his keen tactical and strategic sense was matched only by his courage and martial skill. One by one, Settra brought the other great cities of Nehekhara to heel, leading his legions from the front where he could sate his own battle-lust and thirst to conquer. First Numas fell, then Zandri surrendered, and with every victory more warriors flocked to his banner. Before long, Settra commanded the largest and most devout army that Nehekhara had ever known. Vast legions of battle-hardened soldiers marched across the land at Settra's command, and no mercy was shown to those who dared opposed his might.

Under Settra's inspired and unparalleled generalship, all the kings of Nehekhara were conquered, forced to swear oaths of fealty, pay tribute and acknowledge Khemri as the pre-eminent city of the land once more. Having subjugated his rivals through bloody conquest, Settra had ended the civil war and the Time of Strife.

NEHEKHARA PROSPERS

Few rivals emerged to oppose the great king, and those who did were crushed mercilessly, either at his own hands, or by those of the Herald Nekaph, his imposing champion. Settra's agents would root out and quell any trace of dissent and the merest hint of rebellion that threatened the stability of their lord's realm, and soon none dared to even think of defying the King of Khemri. Thereafter, Settra reigned as the undisputed king of not just Khemri, but of all Nehekhara, and for many decades he suffered no challenge to his rule.

Though Settra was a ruthless and tyrannical ruler, Khemri, and indeed the whole of Nehekhara, entered a golden age of prosperity under his rule. The war-ravaged cities were quickly restored, and many grand monuments were erected to not just the gods, but now also to the honour of Settra. Mighty legions of soldiers were raised to secure Nehekhara's ever-expanding borders and repel the many mutated monsters and savage barbarians that had sunk their claws into the Great Land during the Time of Strife.

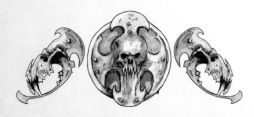

Yet Settra was not content with merely restoring the kingdoms of his ancestors. The armies of Nehekhara spread far and wide, conquering the surrounding lands and enslaving their tribes. Settra's war fleets ravaged realms across the seas, and his armies brought the terror of the Priest King of Khemri to many distant lands. Foreign cities fell, faraway lands were conquered and vast riches were brought back to the Great Land from as far afield as the jungles of Lustria. Nehekhara reached the peak of its power and influence during the reign of Settra, and his name was feared across half the world.

THE UNREACHABLE VISION

There was nothing that could stay Settra's hunger for war, nor his thirst for conquest, and for many years the armies of Nehekhara swept across the world. Settra's vast kingdom stretched across the lands, but for all his victories and accomplishments, the Priest King was unsatisfied. It is said that in the fortieth year of his reign, with his body beginning to show the first signs of old age and frailty, Settra stood in the peaks of the Black Mountains, upon the very edge of his empire, and surveyed all that he had conquered. He then turned and gazed upon the distant lands that lay on the other side of the mountain and roared in anger. It was with bitter disappointment that Settra realised that even if he lived for a hundred years, there would still be realms beyond his grasp.

Settra simmered with rage, for he knew that one day he would be defeated, not by a mortal foe, nor by any superior army – for surely there were none – but by the cruel passage of time and his own mortality. Settra knew that his dreams of global conquest were unreachable in his mortal lifespan, and though the fires of ambition still burned brightly within his heart, his body would wither and fail him before he could see his vision fulfilled. Worse, Settra recognised that death might rob him of all he had achieved: his lands, his people, and his power. Over the following months he became ever more obsessed, demanding audiences with the wisest priests and scholars in the land to discuss how the intolerable problem of his mortality might be overcome. In his arrogance, he vowed that the grave would not claim him, and set in motion events that would forever change his kingdom.

THE MORTUARY CULT

Settra became obsessed with unlocking the secrets of immortality so that he could rule over his lands for all eternity. In his quest for ever-lasting life, Settra founded the Mortuary Cult and demanded that his wisest and most powerful priests devote their efforts to discovering the secrets of preventing his passing. The priests of Khemri did as Settra bade them, and for years they brewed potions, recited incantations and travelled into unknown lands in search of the secret that would overcome death.

In their research, the priests learned much, and they used their powers to extend Settra's life far beyond its natural span. However, they could not halt the passage of time indefinitely – they were merely postponing the inevitability of death while their lord's mortal body became ever more frail. The priests of the Mortuary Cult were naturally reluctant to reveal these limitations to Settra, whose wrath was legendary, and continued to search in vain for a way to accomplish their appointed task.

The priests journeyed for many years throughout the world. They studied all aspects of death, and over the years they learned much, and their powers grew. Using their arcane knowledge, the priests extended the length of their own lives, even as they continued their work. They learned how to preserve a corpse from decay, until the art of mummification had become very elaborate indeed. With the passing of the years, the hierophants of the Mortuary Cult had even begun to experiment with harnessing the Winds of Magic – the power of the gods themselves.

Though they made incredible progress, it was to no avail; true immortality lay beyond their power. Great was Settra's wrath, for though the priests' magic kept him alive far beyond the span of a mortal Man, they could not prevent his death. However, the Mortuary Cult had devised a vast lore

of magical incantations and rituals, which they claimed could bridge the gap between the mortal world and the Realm of Souls. They believed that with careful preparation and the proper incantations, it might be possible for the dead to return to life in imperishable bodies – though it may take many centuries to perfect and perform the necessary rituals. Left with no other choice, Settra commanded that a vast burial tomb be constructed for his body to rest within until the Mortuary Cult finished their work and he could be reborn into the eternal existence he so craved.

THE PYRAMID OF SETTRA

As Settra lay dying, full of anger and pride to his last breath, the priests of the Mortuary Cult promised him a golden paradise that, upon his awakening, he would rule for millions of years. When the king perished, it was with a curse on his lips. Powerful incantations were intoned over his corpse and he was embalmed in a great ritual. Preserved against decay, the body of Settra was entombed within a mighty sarcophagus in the heart of a majestic pyramid of shining white stone. The monument was so bright that it hurt mortal eyes just to look upon it. The pyramid was vast and it towered over the city of Khemri. It was the largest and most magnificent monument ever created in Nehekhara, for no simple cairn would befit a king as mighty and powerful as Settra. All of his treasures, along with his most loyal servants and bodyguards, were also interred within his pyramid. Settra's mighty legions, which had carved out his realm at his behest, were arrayed deep beneath it in colossal tomb pits. Loyal even unto death, these soldiers were buried alive in preparation for the Day of Awakening when Settra would arise and lead them to war once more. At the head of the funeral procession strode Nekaph, Settra's most loyal servant, mummified at the right-hand side of his beloved king, in order to serve him in the next life.

For thousands of years afterwards, the priests of Khemri tended the funeral flames outside the sealed tomb, nurturing Settra's immortal spirit with sacrifice and incantations in preparation for the Day of Awakening. No tomb before or since has ever had such powerful hieroglyphs of warding and incantations of protection heaped upon it. During this time, the priests of the Mortuary Cult continued to develop their understanding of magical incantations in the hopes of finally unlocking the secrets of immortality and of bringing about the time of Settra's resurrection.

"Hail to the mighty Tomb Guard who stand before me, you who will stand watch over me for all eternity. For I, Settra, Lord and first Priest King of Khemri, will awaken to command you in the paradise that awaits us. Hail to the Ushabti and sphinx who stand sentinel beside the monuments of the king. Hail to the commanders of my army, leading forth your regiments to join me in eternity. Hail to the warriors of my legions; make ready your weapons and fill the air with the sound of your worship. Your standards are pleasing to my sight and that of the gods. See how the light of Ptra shines upon them. Remember them gleaming this day, as you enter the darkness of the tomb. Fear not what we must do, for we are the glory of Khemri and shall rise again to fulfil our manifest destiny of ruling this world. There are great deeds that remain undone, enemies yet to conquer and raptures yet to rejoice in. So as it is written, so shall it be done. I, Settra, have proclaimed it – let none dare oppose my will."

– Inscription on the Great Obelisk of Khemri.

THE TIME OF KINGS

Following Settra's death, many dynasties came and went. However, without Settra's stern control and merciless leadership, no single Priest King had the ability to rule over all of Nehekhara. Thus, the individual cities vied and competed with each other over riches and status. Though Nehekhara did not revert to the all-out civil wars of the Time of Strife, skirmishes between neighbouring cities were not unheard of. During this centuries-long era, known as the Time of Kings, the borders of Nehekhara were as changing as the shifting dunes. What existed was a feudal state where power and territory were decided by strength of arms. A king was only as powerful as the size of his armies, and so vast legions were raised with each passing decade.

Though the expansion of the Great Land did not proceed at the same pace as it had during the reign of Settra, every now and then a warrior-king would extend his realm, either by conquering his neighbours or by pacifying some of the savage lands surrounding Nehekhara. Armies of highly disciplined warriors and fearsome chariots warred against the Priest Kings' enemies. In the west, the crude desert nomads were subjugated and their chieftains enlightened by the great civilisation of Nehekhara. In the north and the south, the Priest Kings fought many battles against tribes of greenskins, barbaric men and crocodilian lizard-warriors. These wars brought much wealth to Nehekhara, and slave gangs toiled like ants, hauling their prizes back to the necropolises. Gold was taken from the strongholds of the bearded mountain-dwellers, precious jewels from reptilian temple-cities, exotic stone from as far away as distant Cathay, and fresh slaves from the primitive lands to the north that would one day become known as the Empire. Almost the entirety of this conquered wealth was spent in raising larger legions of soldiers and in the construction of ever-more elaborate tombs.

THE MORTUARY CULT GROWS

All the Priest Kings of Nehekhara shared the same lust for worldly wealth and power, and had the same ambition to defy death and rule for all eternity. However, just as with Settra, none could escape death's embrace, so they maintained the Mortuary Cult in order to reawaken them after their passing. During this time, the power and influence of the Mortuary Cult grew. The first generation of priests, whose skills were comparatively rudimentary, died after prolonging their lives far beyond their natural span. They passed on their knowledge to the next generation who exceeded them in both wisdom and expertise. In this way, the Mortuary Cult's skill accumulated until the fifth generation of priests discovered the secrets of binding their souls into their bodies and did not die. After long years of perseverance and endless research, they had finally unlocked the secrets of eternal life, and though they had not perfected the necessary incantations, the ability to awaken the deceased kings from the sleep of death was almost in their grasp as well.

However, the priesthood, whose members had become known as the Liche Priests, were very careful to keep the secrets of their magical lore to themselves. They had gained unprecedented power and enjoyed a dominion over the lands of Nehekhara second only to that of the royalty themselves, and they were reluctant to give that status up. The Liche Priests reasoned that, so long as the Priest Kings had need of the Mortuary Cult to reawaken them into a golden paradise, nothing would change and they could officiate in perpetuity. Whilst the Liche Priests continued to develop their lore of magical incantations, they witnessed the rise and fall of dynasties, and still they did not die. However, as the centuries passed by, the Liche Priests began to discover the unpleasant difference between eternal life and eternal youth.

THE NECROPOLISES

Nehekhara became a society completely obsessed with death and immortality. Deities such as Djaf, the god of the dead, and Usirian, the god of the Underworld, became as widely worshipped as Ptra, the king of the gods. Skulls and skeletons became common symbols of immortality and everlasting life, and such motifs were emblazoned on the

shields, banners and chariots of the Priest Kings' armies. Heroic warriors were rewarded not with riches and luxuries in life, but with the promise of mummification upon death and the chance of sharing in their lord's eternal rule. It was not just the culture of Nehekhara that changed as the Mortuary Cult grew in power; as the Nehekharans' obsession with death flourished, the architecture and landscape of the Great Land irrevocably changed as well.

Every Priest King demanded that his pyramid outdo the efforts of his predecessors in order to prove his superiority. Though none had the audacity to surpass the majesty of the Great Pyramid of Settra, ever-bigger monuments were raised to honour the achievements of the kings. Titanic statues were carved to stand guard over their remains, keeping them secure through all eternity. Before long, all efforts of the people were expended in building and maintaining the necropolises. Necrotects directed the construction as Liche Priests oversaw the mummification rituals that the Priest Kings believed would one day lead to their resurrection. Soon, lesser nobles demanded similar rites and had tombs of their own constructed beside the royal pyramids. Over centuries, as hundreds of royal lines and their armies were entombed, the shining necropolises of the dead outgrew the now meagre-looking dwellings of the living. No expense was spared in paving the path for immortality, and the splendour, wealth and power of Nehekhara was breathtaking to behold.

However, none could imagine that all this majesty would be destroyed by a single man…

THE TREACHERY OF NAGASH

The fall of Nehekhara, and the tragic destruction of its people, was brought about by the ambition of a twisted priest named Nagash. As the firstborn son of King Khetep of Khemri, Nagash was destined to serve in the Mortuary Cult whilst his younger brother, Thutep, ascended to rule following their father's death. Nagash was an exceptionally gifted student, and due to his talents and heritage he quickly became one of Khemri's High Priests, but this did not sate his thirst for power. Filled with pride and greed, Nagash coveted the throne held by his brother and set into motion a plot to seize the crown for himself. Nagash began to corrupt the religious incantations of the Mortuary Cult, and he gathered together a dozen like-minded acolytes, of which a cruel noble named Arkhan was the foremost. One night, as the clouds covered the moon, Nagash murdered Thutep's bodyguard before entombing the young king alive within the Great Pyramid of their father. The next morning, blood still staining his hands, Nagash placed himself on the throne, and none dared confront him.

THE ARCH-NECROMANCER
The reign of Nagash was a time of terror for all the people of Nehekhara. The usurper king sought to increase his own power by means of devilish sorcery; a blasphemy that the people of Nehekhara felt certain would incur the wrath of the gods. Nagash had learned the art of Dark Magic from a cabal of shipwrecked Dark Elves, captured and imprisoned within his father's pyramid on the eve of his funeral. Nagash tortured the pale-skinned foreigners until they divulged the secrets of their mystical powers, and he proved to be an apt pupil indeed. After only a few years, Nagash had surpassed his tutors' powers, and he destroyed them in a deadly magical duel as they tried to escape.

Nagash began to experiment with necromancy, combining his mastery of Dark Magic with his knowledge of death from the Mortuary Cult. He committed his findings into nine accursed tomes – the Books of Nagash – the most powerful source of necromantic magic in the world. One of Nagash's chief successes was the creation of the cursed Elixir of Life. With it, Nagash had finally unlocked the secret of eternal youth. He allowed Arkhan, his trusted vizier, and his other principal lieutenants, to imbibe the elixir. It granted them immortality and incredible strength but, unable to recreate the potion themselves, they were little more than slaves to Nagash's sinister will.

THE BLACK PYRAMID
To increase his power and maintain dominance over the land, Nagash ordered the building of a vast black pyramid. Whilst the populace of Khemri believed this to be just another burial tomb, it was in fact a structure that would channel and harness the Winds of Magic to Nagash's every whim.

The pyramid became Nagash's obsession, and its construction quickly drained Khemri's resources, forcing the necromancer to wage war to capture building material and replenish his workforce. Nagash demanded great quantities of gold and slaves from other cities to be sent in tribute to Khemri. That which was not given freely was taken by force, and several cities were brutally conquered by Nagash.

Marble the colour of midnight was brought from afar, and innumerable slaves toiled day and night for fifty years until the Black Pyramid of Nagash towered above all other monuments in the whole of Nehekhara. Such was Nagash's arrogance that he had built for himself a tomb that dwarfed even the Great Pyramid of Settra. The broken corpses of countless slaves were built into its foundations, and mystic sigils of power were woven into the Black Pyramid's walls. Even in the baking desert sun, the pyramid was cold to the touch, and not even starlight reflected off its magic-saturated surface. Upon its completion, the Winds of Magic blew more strongly across Nehekhara, and Nagash's mastery of Dark Magic and necromancy increased ten-fold. However, the tribute exacted by Khemri was so great that the poverty-wracked cities of Nehekhara had begun to fall into ruin. Eventually, the other Priest Kings rallied against the tyranny of Khemri. They refused to submit to Nagash any longer, and they began to draw their plans against him.

THE WAR OF THE DEAD
To face the defiant Priest Kings, Nagash used his infernal powers to raise a legion of Skeleton Warriors. This was the first time that the dead were made to walk at the will of another, and the horror of it caused many mortal soldiers to flee before the Undead armies. City after city fell before Nagash, and though the living warriors of Nehekhara fought bravely, every soldier who fell only served to swell the ranks of the Undead. Nagash believed it was only a matter of time before the Priest Kings relented and bent their knees in supplication once more, but his arrogance was to prove his undoing, for he underestimated both their resolve and pride. After many long years, the remaining Priest Kings threw all their strengths and hopes into one final gambit, and the combined armies of seven kings marched upon Khemri.

It was not only flesh and blood warriors who besieged Khemri, for beside the Priest Kings' armies strode towering statues. Faced with destruction by Nagash's sorcery, the Mortuary Cult had finally decided to take action and put their centuries of magical research into practice on the battlefield. In a grand ritual, they summoned the spirits of ancient heroes from the Realm of Souls and bound them into the numerous statues that lined the passageways of the necropolises. The god-like Ushabti, towering Necrolith Colossi and powerful Khemrian Warsphinxes were awakened, ready to be directed to war. With creations such as these fighting at their side, the living warriors of Nehekhara were emboldened, and they crashed into the Undead legions with devastating force.

After a titanic battle, Nagash's forces were defeated by the Army of the Seven Kings. Khemri was besieged, and then sacked. Nagash's immortal lieutenants, who had taken refuge in the cursed Black Pyramid, were dragged out of their sarcophagi into the sunlight one by one, and executed by the vengeful Priest Kings. However, Nagash managed to escape before the Priest Kings found his tomb thanks to the sacrifice of Arkhan, who stalled the attackers long enough for his master to flee. With a curse on his lips, Nagash vowed to turn the entire world into a kingdom of the dead, and travelled north to plot his revenge.

ALCADIZAAR THE CONQUEROR

For hundreds of years, the Priest Kings continued to rule Nehekhara, but the corruption of Nagash had forever tainted the land, and it never truly recovered. The individual city rulers had exhausted their populace in overthrowing Nagash, and they now had to contend with famines, civil wars and marauding barbarians from distant lands. The treachery of Nagash had also tarnished the authority of the royal lines, and it was not until several centuries later that a truly powerful king arose. Alcadizaar, a ruler the likes of which had not been seen since the days of Settra, ascended to the rule of Khemri. Under his wise and charismatic leadership, Alcadizaar bound the Great Cities under his rule, and Nehekhara began to prosper once more.

THE CURSE OF LAHMIA

The treachery of Nagash was hard to forget, and since his Reign of Terror, the Mortuary Cult was watched closely. The Liche Priests were forbidden from deviating from their age-old lore of incantations, which had remained unchanged for centuries. However, the lords of the city of Lahmia hungered for power over their rivals. They saw in Nagash's sorcery the means not only to dominate all of Nehekhara, but also the chance to live forever and sever their dependence on the Mortuary Cult. To this end, they

THE REALM OF SOULS

The Realm of Souls is the revered afterlife of the ancient Nehekharans. It was believed that upon death, the deceased's spirit would enter the Realm of Souls – also known as the Underworld or the Netherworld. Here the Kings of Nehekhara would reside in fantastic palaces until such time as a golden paradise worthy of their status was prepared, whereupon they would rule for a million years. It would be filled with all their servants, soldiers and worldly possessions, and so these were necessarily buried beside their monarch upon his death.

However, not all inhabitants in the Realm of Souls would be afforded such luxury, for in the lowest levels, the cursed and the damned would be subject to an eternity of torture for their sins. Only the wretches, the unworthy and the traitors of Nehekharan society were condemned thus, and the idea that those of noble blood could be damned to such a fate was unthinkable.

The Liche Priests of the Mortuary Cult believe that their magical powers originate from the Realm of Souls. With the proper incantations, the Liche Priests are able to summon forth the spirits of deceased warriors from this mystical plain and bind them into corporeal bodies to fight for Nehekhara once more.

stole one of the blasphemous Books of Nagash from the Black Pyramid, and over the course of centuries they secretly become adept practitioners of necromancy. The queen of Lahmia, Neferata, embraced the malign magic and used her powers to consort with daemonic entities. She created a tainted version of Nagash's elixir, extending her life indefinitely, yet cursing herself for all eternity. Not possessing the skill or knowledge of Nagash, Neferata and her court were struck by an unquenchable thirst for mortal blood. Lahmia had become the birthplace of the Vampires – fell creatures whose individual strength and unholy power were greater than that of a dozen men.

Fearful that necromancy would bring about the wrath of the gods, King Alcadizaar made war on the tainted Vampire queen. Alcadizaar gathered legions from every other Nehekharan city and forged them into a single massed army that he led against Lahmia. Thousands of chariots raced across the land ahead of vast regiments of archers, mighty phalanxes of spearmen and batallions of giant war-statues. Against such a host, not even the accursed Vampires could prevail, and the power of Lahmia was smashed. The pale queen fled, accompanied by those she had embraced into her cursed vampiric existence.

THE DEAD RETURN

Unbeknownst to the Vampires, they had been guided by the implacable will of Nagash since their creation. Residing far away in his fortress, Nagashizzar, amid the mountains to the north-east of Nehekhara, the arch-necromancer recognised the spawn of his own ancient evil and was gladdened by the corruption of Lahmia. Here were worthy champions, their damnation a tribute to his dark genius. Drawing them to him, Nagash welcomed the Vampires, and they became his dark captains. Through them, Nagash began a new offensive against Nehekhara, and the two sides fought numerous battles – the outcomes of which would pave the way for the necromancer's inevitable return.

Beside the Vampires came the dead warriors of a vast host, Skeletons drawn from the tombs and cairns of the northern lands by the power of Nagash's sorcery. Nagash resurrected his trusted servant, Arkhan the Black, who won many victories in his master's name. War assailed Nehekhara for years on end, and the land was irredeemably scarred. However, Alcadizaar was the greatest general of his age, and he led the unified army of Nehekhara against Nagash's evil for all their long years of battle. Under his leadership, the living legions of Nehekhara never yielded, and finally, during the Battle of the Golden Skull, the Undead hordes of Nagash were repulsed from Nehekhara. The Vampires scattered throughout the world to escape destruction, and without their magic and leadership, their armies of Skeletons crumbled. Nagash had been defeated. There was much rejoicing throughout Nehekhara, though the evil sorcerer himself still walked the land.

THE VENGEANCE OF NAGASH

Such was Nagash's bitterness, so great the potency of his thwarted ambition, that he chose to end all life in Nehekhara rather than see anyone else hold power over the land. He polluted the Great Vitae River, poisoning it until it turned thick and dark, tainting the lands that relied on its life-bringing waters. Forever after it was known as the Great

Mortis River. Pestilence and disease ran rampant across the Great Land. Within a few weeks, those who had succumbed to the terrible plagues outnumbered the living. The city streets were choked with corpses as fully nine-tenths of the Nehekharan population perished. Mourning for his lost people, Alcadizaar sat upon his throne as his kingdom was destroyed – for all his skill at arms, he was powerless. Nagash's Undead forces marched upon Khemri, brushing aside the city's plague-ravaged guard with impunity and walking past the fortress walls and siege-barracks unchallenged. His Skeleton Warriors broke into Khemri's royal palace and dragged Alcadizaar away to rot in a dungeon cell. For the first time in centuries, Nagash sat upon the throne of Khemri.

However, Nagash did not linger in Khemri for long. Filled with insane visions of power, he returned to Nagashizzar and began to cast the greatest and most terrifying spell ever conceived. He intended to enact the Great Ritual, a spell powerful enough to resurrect every corpse across the globe and bind them under his control. With them, Nagash would command an unstoppable army of the dead that he could use to conquer the entire world. To power his Great Ritual, he consumed vast quantities of warpstone and summoned all the energies stored within his cursed Black Pyramid. As Nagash chanted within his fortress, the sky began to darken for hundreds of miles around and the ground shook. As his spell reached its crescendo, a great wave of power surged from the sorcerer's body, washing over the lands of Nehekhara and

stealing the life from everything in its path. Crops shrivelled and animals perished within seconds. The last people of Nehekhara fell to the ground, their skin withering as if they had aged a century in the blink of an eye.

Within minutes, there was not a single living creature in the entirety of Nehekhara. Such was Nagash's execration of Alcadizaar, who had thwarted his plans for so long, that he spared the imprisoned king to witness the horrifying fate that had befallen his former kingdom.

THE DEATH OF NAGASH

Whilst the Great Ritual scoured the land of life, some things remained undetected far beneath Nagashizzar. While Nagash was channelling his great spell, drunk with magical power and lost in dreams of triumph, Alcadizaar, the last mortal king of Nehekhara, was mysteriously freed from his prison below Nagashizzar by a group of hunched, heavily cloaked, rat-like creatures. A powerful blade, made of purest warpstone, was pushed into his hands, and the emaciated king stumbled into Nagash's throne room just as the sorcerer was reaching the climax of his mighty ritual. Through sheer force of will, Alcadizaar summoned the strength to swing his baleful sword and cut the hated necromancer down. As Nagash died, the energies of his accursed spell spiralled out of his control and swept across his homeland. Alcadizaar, filled with horror at the obscenities he had seen and having witnessed the death of his beloved realm, then faded from history.

THE TOMB KINGS AWAKEN

As Nagash's powerful sorceries coursed across Nehekhara, countless corpses stirred and rose, animated solely by the dark will of the necromancer. With his destruction, their source of animus vanished and they fell like marionettes whose strings had been mysteriously cut. Nagash's foul magic also penetrated the tombs of the kings and reverberated throughout the charnel pits of the dead cities. However, protected and shielded to a degree by the wards and incantations placed upon their pyramids and necropolises, Nagash's spell affected the long-dead kings and their buried legions differently.

After centuries of entombment, the stiffened corpses of monarchs and heroes awoke. The mummified kings rose from their resting places. Legions of Skeleton Warriors burst forth from their sand-filled tomb pits, ready to do their liege's bidding. Due to the incantations of preservation performed on their embalmed bodies, the Tomb Kings awoke from their long journey through the Realm of Souls with their memories and faculties intact. They emerged from their tombs in horror. Where the ancient kings had been promised eternal life in a paradise where they would rule supreme, they instead awoke to find themselves clad in desiccated flesh and rotten vestments, with their cities shattered, their lands desolate and their kingdoms all but destroyed – little more than ruins poking out from beneath the sand dunes.

THE WAR OF THE KINGS

There had been countless kings during the long history of Nehekhara. The fires of ambition and pride that had driven them in life still resided in their ancient bodies, and they instantly set out to reclaim their empires as best they could. Kings who were great and powerful in life, who had reigned unchallenged for centuries, now awoke from death in a land where they were but one amongst hundreds. All believed the right to rule the land was solely theirs, and none would relinquish their perceived power. Dynasties that were built upon the shoulders of more powerful monarchs were forced to confront their founders, and there were long battles in the necropolises as king fought king. Undying legions arose at their command, and many thousands of Skeleton Warriors were destroyed as the Undead Tomb Kings struggled for supremacy. Of all the tombs and pyramids, only one remained silent and untouched by the fighting – the Great Pyramid of Settra the Imperishable. The wards heaped on the white burial monument had protected the mummified corpse of Settra from Nagash's tainted sorcery, and its occupants still slumbered in the sleep of death, oblivious to the tumult of battle taking place outside the pyramid walls.

As the battles raged, the Liche Priests looked on. Their bodies, already extended far beyond their natural span, were unaffected by Nagash's spell. They had survived the rise and fall of Nagash, whose sorcerous power they could not match, but it looked like the warring Tomb Kings were going to destroy what remained of Nehekhara. The head of the Mortuary Cult, Grand Hierophant Khatep, oldest and wisest of the Liche Priests, took it upon himself to restore order. As king smote king, Khatep broke the seals to Settra's pyramid and began to recite the incantation of awakening.

SETTRA AWAKENS

In Khemri, the battles between rival kings lasted for days before the tomb of Settra opened, and the mightiest of all the kings of Nehekhara strode out into the blazing sunlight at the head of thousands of his warriors.

In undeath, Settra hungered for the domination of his fellow Tomb Kings, and he would suffer no rival to his rule. Settra waded into the carnage. His Herald, Nekaph, stood as ever by his side. Together, they led Settra's elite Tomb Guard and quickly carved a path through the rival Skeleton legions. Settra struck down dozens of lesser Tomb Kings who stood against him, powdering their bones to dust and destroying them utterly. Not even Arkhan the Black, with his command of dark sorcery, could prevail against Settra's strength of arms, and he was forced to flee Khemri. Before long, all the Tomb Kings bowed their heads to Settra the Imperishable – the undisputed ruler of all Nehekhara.

THE REIGN OF MILLIONS OF YEARS

Settra returned to his throne room and commanded the Liche Priests to explain to him why the awakening had gone awry, and so long before the right and proper time. Settra's fury was great; his cities were in ruins, his treasures had been plundered and much of his kingdom had been lost to foreign invaders. The golden paradise he was promised did not exist, and worst of all, it appeared as if the ancient gods had abandoned Nehekhara. Grand Hierophant Khatep cowered before the outraged king and told the history of Nehekhara since his passing over two thousand years before. As best he could, Khatep told Settra of the spell that the foul Nagash had cast, cursing Nehekhara for all time.

Settra listened with a barely controlled rage simmering within him. Once he had learned all he could from Khatep, he commanded that the Tomb Kings return to their eternal rest. The Liche Priests were given the duty of watching over the tombs and of awakening his vassal kings as needed. Settra vowed that he would stay vigilant, taking stock of the world and waging war as was his wont. Never again would he slumber, lest his kingdom slide into ruin.

Settra set about restoring his former empire without delay. In particular, he watched for the return of the hated Nagash, who had cursed his realm, for he knew that the necromancer might yet reappear in the world and that Nagash's sorcery could still threaten his immortality.

So it was that Nehekhara became the Land of the Dead and Settra the Imperishable renewed his rulership, which would become known as the Reign of Millions of Years.

THE LAND OF THE DEAD

Whilst the land of Nehekhara was once fertile, populous and prosperous, it is now a desolate kingdom. In addition to the centuries of war and neglect, the lands were forever tainted by the enchantments of Nagash's Great Ritual. The Land of the Dead is a now a ghost-haunted realm where countless unquiet spirits and elementals flit around great mortuary temples and dark tombs. Their cries can be heard screaming in the wind as they cross the vast tracts of Nehekhara's baking deserts, preying on those foolish enough to enter the cursed land in search of treasure.

Nehekhara is a hostile realm where the searing heat of the desert sun is the least of a wandering traveller's worries. The waters of the Great Mortis River are poisonous and blood-coloured, providing no relief to the thirsty. There are regions of quicksand that can swallow regiments whole and choking sandstorms that strip the flesh from bones in mere seconds. Whirlwinds of dust, skulls and ravenous desert insects scour through the land, and rivers of flesh-eating beetles crawl across the desert, consuming everything in their path. There are vast plains of bones and skulls that come to life without warning, skeletal fingers reaching up to drag anything alive on the surface into a sandy grave below. A few oases still exist, scattered throughout the arid desert, but they are all tainted; instead of fresh water they are filled with bubbling pools of blood. Most are the abodes of foul monsters, and those that are not are lined with parched, malevolent trees that strangle their victims and suck every drop of moisture from their bodies.

Nehekhara is a wilderness of ever shifting sands, a land of constantly changing topography. There are waterfalls of sand that defy the passage of time and flow backwards. There exist dunes and basins large enough to accommodate entire armies, and many of the Tomb King's legions lie beneath the surface in such places – awaiting the magical incantations of Liche Priests to awaken them from their deathly slumber. A sandstorm might unearth a monolithic statue, or even an entire buried city, lost and forgotten under the dunes, only to be engulfed and concealed again a few days later. Such hidden places are said to include the mysterious City of Bronze, a complex rumoured to be covered in glyphs carved by beings older than Nehekhara itself.

In addition to open deserts, where sand stretches as far as the eye can see, there are vast necropolises and numerous places where one can hardly move for all the statues and sculptures, each covered with grisly images of death. These monuments are vaster and grander than anything the Old World can boast, and foremost amongst them are towering figures resembling the great kings and angry gods of Nehekhara – fearsome statues that come to life and smite trespassers with impunity.

When the Tomb Kings awoke, they ordered their Undead minions to rebuild the cities of old and fill them with the markets, wares, boats, and other things that they remembered from life. As few trees grow in the Land of the Dead, many of these things are fashioned from stone, gold or fused bones. Skeletal men walk the lands fulfilling seemingly pointless jobs such as fetching stagnant water,

harvesting crops long since withered or else rowing barges across the Great Mortis River. Armies of Skeletons are forever patrolling the borders of their realm as they did in life, relentlessly striding across the arid landscape in search of enemies and intruders.

Numerous Undead creatures wander the deep desert, from swarms of small but deadly desert scorpions to giant centipedes, each the size of a sphinx. Great flocks of Carrion circle high above, and packs of ravenous sand sharks swim beneath the surface of the dunes. In the centuries since Nagash's Great Ritual, many foul monsters have been drawn to the magically tainted realm. There are now Manticores, Cockatrices and even Dragons inhabiting the Nehekharan desert. Nomadic bandits make a living by plundering the tombs of ancient kings, and marauding Orc tribes continuously rampage across the Land of the Dead in search of battle and plunder. Nehekhara may be a barren realm, but it is far from empty or uninhabited.

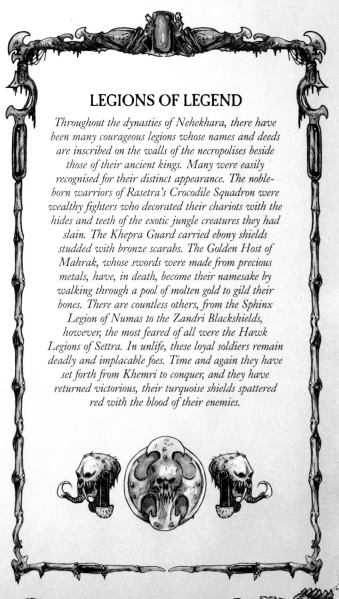

LEGIONS OF LEGEND

Throughout the dynasties of Nehekhara, there have been many courageous legions whose names and deeds are inscribed on the walls of the necropolises beside those of their ancient kings. Many were easily recognised for their distinct appearance. The noble-born warriors of Rasetra's Crocodile Squadron were wealthy fighters who decorated their chariots with the hides and teeth of the exotic jungle creatures they had slain. The Khepra Guard carried ebony shields studded with bronze scarabs. The Golden Host of Mahrak, whose swords were made from precious metals, have, in death, become their namesake by walking through a pool of molten gold to gild their bones. There are countless others, from the Sphinx Legion of Numas to the Zandri Blackshields, however, the most feared of all were the Hawk Legions of Settra. In unlife, these loyal soldiers remain deadly and implacable foes. Time and again they have set forth from Khemri to conquer, and they have returned victorious, their turquoise shields spattered red with the blood of their enemies.

The Great Ocean

The Land of the Dead

N

Plain of Bones

The Straits of Nagash

Nagashizzar

The Sour Sea

The Marshes of Madness

The Badlands and The Empire

Black Water

The Sea of Dread

The Bitter Sea

LAHMIA
The Cursed City

Devil's Backbone

Gulf of Fear

LYBARAS
Tomb City of Asaph

The Cursed Jungle

Doom Glade Swamp

Temple of Skulls

MAHRAK
City of Decay

Battle of the Old Gods

Crater of the Waking Dead

Jungle

RASETRA
Fortress of Vengeful Souls

Red Cloud Mountain

Mortis Tarn

Doom Mountain

Mount Arachnos

Lost Plateau

Battle of the Mighty Flame

Charnel Valley

NUMAS
The Scarab City

Battle of The Salt Plain

Ash River

QUATAR
Palace of Corpses

KHEMRI
City of Kings

Springs of Eternal Life

Great Mortis River

Black Pyramid of Nagash

BHAGAR
The Eternal Necropolis

KA-SABAR
Temple of Sorrow

Swamp of Terror

The Battle of the Golden Skull

Black Tower of Arkhan

The Southlands

ZANDRI
Fleetport of Terror

Pools of Despair

The Cracked Land

Shifting Sands

Great Sandy Desert

Jungle

BEL ALIAD
City of Dust

to Araby

Great Desert of Araby

Battle of the Bitter Wind

EL-KALABAD

Gulf of Medes

18

REALM OF THE DEAD

The sprawling necropolises of the Tomb Kings are skull-engraved monuments of death that dominate the skyline of Nehekhara. Within are dozens of Tomb Kings, countless generations spanning several dynasties. However, it is rare for any city to be ruled by more than a single Tomb King at any one time. When a Tomb King falls in battle, the Liche Priests may awaken another to rule in his stead. Alternativley, a Tomb Prince may ascend to the throne, or the fallen king's remains may be placed within his pyramid to restore his form over several decades. Though the Tomb Kings are immortal and may reign for centuries at a time, all eventually need to return to the sarcophagus in their pyramids to rest. Settra the Imperishable, alone amongst the Tomb Kings, possesses the strength of will needed to remain awake all the time, and he rules eternally from the city of Khemri.

KHEMRI, CITY OF KINGS

Khemri is the jewel in the crown of Nehekhara. It is the oldest, largest, proudest and most powerful of all the ancient cities. The monuments built in this grand necropolis are vast and majestic to behold, crafted by the most skilled Necrotects in the land. Graven images of gods and monsters peer down from every rooftop, and statuary marks the corner of every dust-scattered street. Throughout Nehekhara's long history, the greatest of all the kings were those of Khemri. It became established early on that whoever ruled the City of Kings was the mightiest sovereign in all the Great Land, he to whom the other kings would pledge allegiance and offer tribute.

In the heart of Khemri lies the lavish royal palace in which Settra the Imperishable sits upon a throne made of gold, soul-diamonds and a wealth of other gemstones worth more than the combined treasures of a dozen lesser kings. Beside this court of power looms one of the most magnificent structures ever created by Mankind – Settra's Great Pyramid. Within this ivory edifice, Nehekhara's fearsome legions await the king's command, standing ready to march to war and destroy his enemies. However, even this majestic monument, rising hundreds of times the height of a man, is dwarfed by the Black Pyramid of Nagash – a wonder and a terror to all who behold it, lying silent and ominous on the outskirts of Khemri.

ZANDRI, FLEETPORT OF TERROR

The Tomb Kings' domain is not limited to the endless sands – they also bring war to the seas. The coast around the Mortis delta is filled with the sunken wrecks of numerous pirate ships – fools that have attacked Zandri in the search of untold riches. In the city's harbours at the mouth of the Great Mortis River, ancient barges that writhe with dark energy still float, manned by Skeleton crews who bend their backs at the oars to the resonant boom of drums and the cracks of their taskmaster's whips. Along the waters of the miles-wide Mortis River, and across the Great Ocean to the north, the Tomb Fleets bring the terror of Nehekhara to distant realms. These imposing armadas set out laden with skeletal legions and vengeful rulers thirsty for conquest, and return with blood-slick weapons and recovered treasures, plundered from Nehekhara in ages past.

LYBARAS, TOMB-CITY OF ASAPH

Though smaller than the other cities of Nehekhara, Lybaras is no less a vision of decayed splendour. Vast temple complexes tower into the sky, and every burial pyramid is topped with gold. Lybaras is the resting place of High Queen Khalida, renowned for her enchanting beauty, martial pride and her deep-rooted hatred of Nagash's tainted race of Vampires. Since Khalida's reign and tragic murder, Asaph, goddess of vengeance and magic, has become the city's patron. Carvings of her beloved asps adorn every surface of the city's funeral monuments, and these serpentine engravings constantly writhe across the stonework, hissing at any who walk in their shadow and spying on any who dare explore the streets. Of all Nehekhara's cities, Lybaras has the most independence from Khemri's rule. This is due, in no small part, to its distance and isolation from Settra's court. Lybaras is surrounded on three sides: by the mountain range known as the Devil's Backbone to the west, the Cursed Jungle to the south and the sulphuric waters of the Gulf of Fear to the east. The only negotiable path lies to the north, past the tainted ruins of Lahmia, where the spirits of the damned lurk and feed upon any who enter.

THE CHARNEL VALLEY

The Charnel Valley was known long ago as the Valley of the Kings. At one entrance to the foreboding valley stands the alabaster palace of Quatar, while at the other sits the necropolis of Mahrak, the City of Decay. Throughout the Charnel Valley's entire length stand colossal statues, exquisite representations of powerful gods and mighty kings, carved from the face of the thousand-cubit high valley wall. Few living souls dare to travel into the Charnel Valley, and none have ever returned, for these statues do not sit idly by – they constantly patrol the valley in search of trespassers, crunching the thick carpet of bones and skulls littering the valley floor to dust beneath their heavy footfalls. It is said that the greatest Necrotects of Nehekhara now reside within the Charnel Valley as they work tirelessly to re-sculpt the visages of these magnificent monuments, eroded by centuries of wind-swept sand and battered from endless years of warfare.

THE BLACK TOWER OF ARKHAN

This fell tower was built by Nagash's trusted vizier at the height of the Reign of Terror. Isolated deep in the Cracked Land, the Black Tower offered Arkhan a refuge where he could develop his mastery of Dark Magic. Constructed in union with the accursed Black Pyramid, Arkhan's infernal spire and the lands that surround it are saturated with magic, and many vile things dwell in its shadow. Following Nagash's defeat by the Army of the Seven Kings and Arkhan's mortal-death, the Black Tower was abandoned, and for centuries it remained a haunted place, shunned by all. Only evil spirits stirred inside its catacombs. Upon Arkhan's return to Nehekhara, he raised an army of Skeletons to guard against his Tomb King rivals and carved out a realm of his own. Arkhan rules from the Black Tower, maintaining an uneasy truce with the monarchs of Nehekhara through the power of dark sorcery. Whatever his true motives, Arkhan the Black is a powerful ally for those who can afford his price…

AN AGE OF KINGS

–c.2,500

The Rise of Nehekhara – During this time there were many kings and their names are not remembered, save for Nehek, who founded the city of Khemri. Thereafter, other cities were raised, but the kings warred upon each other and there was much strife in the land.

–2,500

Settra is crowned as the first of the Priest Kings and conquers the entirety of Nehekhara. With his coming, the great rulership of Khemri becomes law, and Nehekhara enters an unprecedented era of prosperity and expansion.

–c.2,460

Following his victory over the Orcs of the Bloody Fang tribe, Settra becomes vexed that he will one day grow old and die. Settra founds the Mortuary Cult and commands its priests to discover the secrets of immortality.

–2390

Settra names Nekaph as his personal champion. Over the following decades Nekaph secures the unconditional surrender of over a dozen foreign cities. Scores more refuse to submit to Settra's rule and are subsequently destroyed.

–2383

The King of Bhagar revolts against Settra's rule. Order is quickly restored when the Herald Nekaph travels to the city and slays the rebellious king.

–2350

Settra perishes, and his body is interred within a magnificent pyramid in preparation for a time when he will arise to his Reign of Millions of Years.

–2350 to –1950

The Time of Kings – Dozens of kings come and pass following the death of Settra. Upon their deaths, they are mummified and entombed in ever more elaborate pyramids along with the still-living soldiery of their legions.

–2,000

The Birth of Nagash.

–1968

A cabal of Dark Elves are driven off course by storms and are shipwrecked in Nehekhara. Nagash captures and imprisons the pale-skinned foreigners and learns the secrets of Dark Magic from them.

–1950 to –1600

The Reign of Terror – Nagash murders his brother and seizes the throne of Khemri. He creates the Elixir of Life to prolong his fading youth and rules his kingdom through dread and fear. During this time, Nagash develops his mastery of sorcery and instructs the building of the Black Pyramid. Following its construction, Nagash and his vizier, Arkhan, raise armies of Skeletons to war against the Priest Kings.

–1600

Nagash is overthrown by the Army of the Seven Kings. Khemri is besieged and then sacked. Arkhan is killed covering his master's retreat. Nagash flees north to plot his revenge.

–1600 to –1200

Dynasties rise and fall, each trying to rebuild their lands following the treachery of Nagash. Nehekhara reverts to a feudal state.

–1563

The royal line of Numas is murdered by Prince Apophas. The populace rebels and Apophas is executed, his bones cursed to the depths of the Underworld.

–1520

Neferata, Queen of Lahmia, recreates the Elixir of Life, birthing the race of Vampires. Neferata's cousin, Queen Khalida of Lybaras, grows suspicious of the Lahmian court, but is slain before she can expose their dark secret.

–c.1200

Alcadizaar the Conquerer is crowned King of Khemri. He binds the entire land of Nehekhara under his charismatic rule and conquers the ancient city of Ka-Sabar from the desert tribes. Nehekhara begins to prosper once more.

–c.1185

Ramhotep, the greatest Necrotect of Nehekhara, finishes construction of the Sepulchre of the Heavens in Quatar. As a reward, the master artisan is mummified alive and interred within this magnificent monument.

–1170

The taint of vampirism is discovered in Lahmia. The entire cursed city is reduced to ruins by Alcadizaar's forces, and the Vampires are forced to flee north to Nagashizzar.

–1163

Nagash returns. He resurrects Arkhan the Black who joins the Vampires in leading a vast army of the dead against the Priest Kings but, led by Alcadizaar, the living prevail against them.

–1152

Plague besets Nehekhara. Nagash comes forth for a second time and the Priest Kings are unable to stop him. Alcadizaar is imprisoned and Nagash sits upon the throne of Khemri.

–1151

The Great Ritual – After consuming vast amounts of warpstone, Nagash casts the great spell of awakening and curses the realm of Nehekhara to undeath. Before the ritual's completion, Nagash is slain by Alcadizaar, mysteriously freed from captivity. The great spell spirals out of control and the Tomb Kings stir from their slumber. Alcadizaar vanishes from history. So ends the living line of Khemrian kings.

–c.1151

The War of the Kings – Bitter fighting wracks Nehekhara as the Tomb Kings battle each other for supremacy. Khatep opens the Great Pyramid of Khemri and awakens Settra, who smites his rivals and brings all under his rule. So begins Settra's Reign of Millions of Years.

–1149

Arkhan the Black, repelled from Khemri by Settra, attacks the city of Bel-Aliad, beginning what Arabyan chroniclers will later call the Wars of Death. For the next thousand years Arkhan raids the lands of the living across the world.

–975

Apophas is reborn as the Cursed Scarab Lord and begins to roam the world in search for the one soul that will release him from his eternal torment.

–917

Nehekhara is invaded by Lizardmen from the Southlands who are searching for lost plaques looted from their temple-cities in ages past. The reptilian warhost smashes aside skeletal armies at both Ka-Sabar and Bhagar as they continue to march ever deeper into the Land of the Dead. They are finally defeated at the City of Kings when Liche Priests focus the rays of the sun through the mirrored prisms atop Khemri's gold-capped pyramids.

–642

The Black Maw tribe of Ogres descends upon the city of Quatar, intent on a feast of bread made from the ground bones of ancient kings. Several tombs are demolished and countless hundreds of Skeleton Warriors are smashed asunder by the Ogre horde, before an army of statues marches out of the Charnel Valley and utterly destroys the invaders.

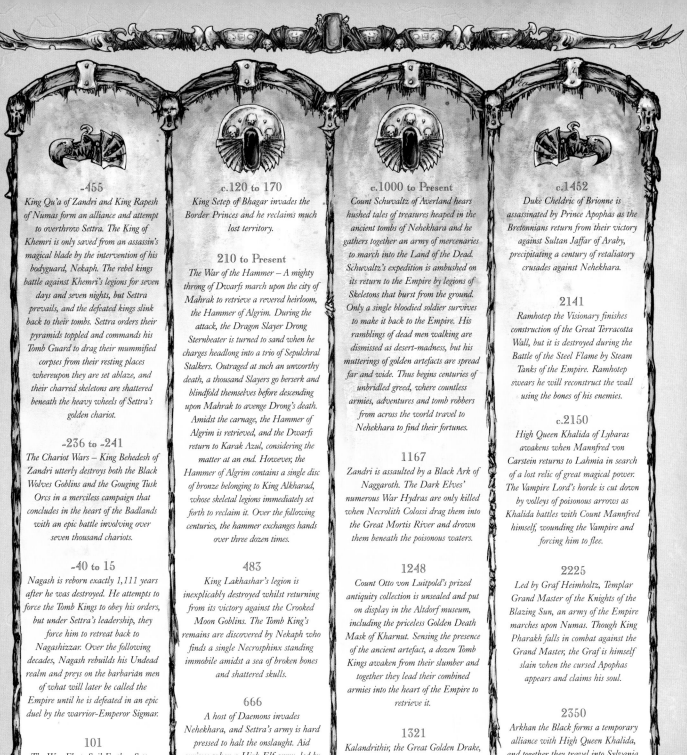

-455

King Qu'a of Zandri and King Rapesh of Numas form an alliance and attempt to overthrow Settra. The King of Khemri is only saved from an assassin's magical blade by the intervention of his bodyguard, Nekaph. The rebel kings battle against Khemri's legions for seven days and seven nights, but Settra prevails, and the defeated kings slink back to their tombs. Settra orders their pyramids toppled and commands his Tomb Guard to drag their mummified corpses from their resting places whereupon they are set ablaze, and their charred skeletons are shattered beneath the heavy wheels of Settra's golden chariot.

-236 to -241

The Chariot Wars – King Behedesh of Zandri utterly destroys both the Black Wolves Goblins and the Gouging Tusk Orcs in a merciless campaign that concludes in the heart of the Badlands with an epic battle involving over seven thousand chariots.

-40 to 15

Nagash is reborn exactly 1,111 years after he was destroyed. He attempts to force the Tomb Kings to obey his orders, but under Settra's leadership, they force him to retreat back to Nagashizzar. Over the following decades, Nagash rebuilds his Undead realm and preys on the barbarian men of what will later be called the Empire until he is defeated in an epic duel by the warrior-Emperor Sigmar.

101

The War Fleets Sail Forth – Settra seeks to restore his dominance of the oceans as well as the lands, and he instructs that his war fleets be rasied and made sea worthy once more.

111

Arkhan the Black returns to Nehekhara. He reclaims the Black Tower and carves out a realm of his own, establishing an uneasy truce with the other Tomb Kings.

c.120 to 170

King Setep of Bhagar invades the Border Princes and he reclaims much lost territory.

210 to Present

The War of the Hammer – A mighty throng of Dwarfs march upon the city of Mahrak to retrieve a revered heirloom, the Hammer of Algrim. During the attack, the Dragon Slayer Drong Sternbeater is turned to sand when he charges headlong into a trio of Sepulchral Stalkers. Outraged at such an unworthy death, a thousand Slayers go berserk and blindfold themselves before descending upon Mahrak to avenge Drong's death. Amidst the carnage, the Hammer of Algrim is retrieved, and the Dwarfs return to Karak Azul, considering the matter at an end. However, the Hammer of Algrim contains a single disc of bronze belonging to King Alkharad, whose skeletal legions immediately set forth to reclaim it. Over the following centuries, the hammer exchanges hands over three dozen times.

483

King Lakhashar's legion is inexplicably destroyed whilst returning from its victory against the Crooked Moon Goblins. The Tomb King's remains are discovered by Nekaph who finds a single Necrosphinx standing immobile amidst a sea of broken bones and shattered skulls.

666

A host of Daemons invades Nehekhara, and Settra's army is hard pressed to halt the onslaught. Aid arrives when a High Elf army, led by Prince Stormrider, offers an alliance. The spears of the Glittering Host and the Golden Army fight side by side, and the Daemons are vanquished before Nagash's Black Pyramid.

873

Rasetra is attacked by the dragon-sized spiders of Mount Arachnos and saved only due to the magical intervention of a mysterious stranger.

c.1000 to Present

Count Schuvaltz of Averland hears hushed tales of treasures heaped in the ancient tombs of Nehekhara and he gathers together an army of mercenaries to march into the Land of the Dead. Schuvaltz's expedition is ambushed on its return to the Empire by legions of Skeletons that burst from the ground. Only a single bloodied soldier survives to make it back to the Empire. His ramblings of dead men walking are dismissed as desert-madness, but his mutterings of golden artefacts are spread far and wide. Thus begins centuries of unbridled greed, where countless armies, adventures and tomb robbers from across the world travel to Nehekhara to find their fortunes.

1167

Zandri is assaulted by a Black Ark of Naggaroth. The Dark Elves' numerous War Hydras are only killed when Necrolith Colossi drag them into the Great Mortis River and drown them beneath the poisonous waters.

1248

Count Otto von Luitpold's prized antiquity collection is unsealed and put on display in the Altdorf museum, including the priceless Golden Death Mask of Kharnut. Sensing the presence of the ancient artefact, a dozen Tomb Kings awaken from their slumber and together they lead their combined armies into the heart of the Empire to retrieve it.

1321

Kalandrithir, the Great Golden Drake, awakens from his millennia-long hibernation in the Worlds Edge Mountains. For reasons unknown, the vast Dragon descends into the Land of the Dead and topples dozens of Quatar's pyramids, obliterating whole dynasties of Tomb Kings whilst they slumber. Kalandrithir continues tearing the necropolis asunder until a Necrolith Colossus shoots the ancient creature through the heart with a single shot from a giant golden bow.

c.1452

Duke Cheldric of Brionne is assassinated by Prince Apophas as the Bretonnians return from their victory against Sultan Jaffar of Araby, precipitating a century of retaliatory crusades against Nehekhara.

2141

Ramhotep the Visionary finishes construction of the Great Terracotta Wall, but it is destroyed during the Battle of the Steel Flame by Steam Tanks of the Empire. Ramhotep swears he will reconstruct the wall using the bones of his enemies.

c.2150

High Queen Khalida of Lybaras awakens when Mannfred von Carstein returns to Lahmia in search of a lost relic of great magical power. The Vampire Lord's horde is cut down by volleys of poisonous arrows as Khalida battles with Count Mannfred himself, wounding the Vampire and forcing him to flee.

2225

Led by Graf Heimholtz, Templar Grand Master of the Knights of the Blazing Sun, an army of the Empire marches upon Numas. Though King Pharakh falls in combat against the Grand Master, the Graf is himself slain when the cursed Apophas appears and claims his soul.

2350

Arkhan the Black forms a temporary alliance with High Queen Khalida, and together they travel into Sylvania. As Khalida smites the Vampire Lord Mandregan, Arkhan recovers the Staff of Nagash from his coffin.

2522 to Present

Settra the Imperishable embarks upon his great purge and begins a new age of conquest, seeking to enlarge his realm to encompass the entire world. The armies of Nehekhara mass behind him and thus the great expansion begins.

THE LEGIONS GO TO WAR

The battles of the Tomb Kings are many, and were a thousand scribes to toil for a thousand years they could not recount them all. Here are just a couple of these epic tales.

THE WAR OF SAND AND SNOW

Settra the Imperishable had ruled as the Undead king of all Nehekhara for over a millennia when an army of marauding tribesmen from the frozen north made landfall on the baking shores of Nehekhara. The barbaric warriors plundered several tombs before the Skeleton Warriors of Settra's legions began to rise from the sands to bar their escape. Even as the Marauders prepared to face this threat, the skies began to darken. The barbarians gazed to the heavens, and a heartbeat later, a cloud of arrows fell amongst them that cut down hundreds of warriors. In the wake of the volley, vast flocks of Carrion descended upon the wounded and the dying, razor-sharp beaks tearing open throats and bellies. The tribe's chieftain, Valgar the Butcher, ordered a savage counter-attack, unleashing packs of bloodthirsty Warhounds that tore the Carrion apart in a frenzied gnashing of teeth. Valgar then redressed his surviving warriors' ranks and prepared to meet the approaching Skeleton battle line.

Axes clashed with spears as the two forces collided, but wherever Valgar fought, the Undead were hewn by his axe or crushed beneath the hooves of his daemonic steed. Despite Valgar's fearsome skill, his forces were vastly outnumbered and his own warriors were growing tired, their strength sapped by the punishing glare of the desert sun. In the distance, Valgar could see a single figure emerge through the heat-haze, a majestic warrior riding forwards on a golden chariot. Valgar raised his rune-covered axe to the air and bellowed a challenge to the new-comer – a challenge that was answered with a rumble of thunder.

That figure was none other than Settra the Imperishable, and he smashed into the invaders with the wrath of ancient gods, driving a bloody path towards Valgar. As the two generals collided, Settra swung his enchanted blade in a mighty arc that decapitated Valgar's daemonic mount in a single blow. Even as Valgar's steed was slain from beneath him, the chieftain's axe glowed with baleful energy, and it was suddenly wreathed in sorcerous flames. The axe bit deep into Settra's chest and set his form ablaze. Before Valgar could enjoy his victory, Settra's body exploded into a ravenous swarm of beetles that stripped the chieftain's flesh from his bones before flying back to the Great Pyramid of Khemri to regenerate the Tomb King's immortal form. Amidst the carnage, Valgar's lieutenant, Khagul Bloodfist, stooped down to pick up Settra's regal crown before rallying the surviving tribesmen and driving a path through the skeletal shield-wall back to the coast. Only a dozen Marauders managed to survive and escape back to their frozen realm, bloodied, but rich beyond their wildest dreams.

SETTRA'S REVENGE

It was a decade before Settra remerged from his sarcophagus, his body restored but his heart burning with the need for vengeance. The men of the north had not only dared to enter his realm, soiling the desert with their barbaric feet, they had

the temerity to face him in battle, even going so far as to strike him down. However, most heinous of all crimes had been the bold act of laying their lowborn hands upon the Crown of Nehekhara – a deed that brought with it a sentence of death. Settra the Imperishable would punish the barbarians for their insolence by staining the snows of their homeland red with their blood.

The King of Nehekhara turned to his Liche Priests and ordered them to awaken his vassal kings; the combined might of Khemri's armies was going to war. Settra's war fleets sailed north, towards the frozen wastelands, laden with legions of Undead soldiers and war-constructs. The King of Nehekhara swore that only when every last gold coin was recovered, and every one of the barbarians who had escaped his wrath a decade ago was slain, would he return to Khemri.

Each of those men had become a chieftain in his own right, with the wealth they brought back from the Land of the Dead securing them much power and many followers. Several had become Champions of Chaos and now they led whole tribes of merciless warriors and mutated monsters.

Settra's warhost collided with the iron-clad Warriors of Chaos across the entire length of the northern lands. Enormous statues strode relentlessly through driving blizzards, and regiments of Skeleton Chariots tirelessly ploughed through snow-drifts in their hunt for the guilty. Untold thousands of men were slaughtered upon the swords and spears of Settra's host as tribe after tribe was destroyed. Dragon Ogres were cut down by powerful Ushabti, Trolls were turned into pillars of sand by Sepulchral Stalkers and grotesque Giants were slain by the monstrous claws of ferocious Necrosphinxes. Driven by Settra's unyielding will, the legions of Nehekhara were unstoppable. Within five years only one of the dozen Mauraders remained alive, and only a single treasure – the Crown of Nehekhara – remained unclaimed. Settra's revenge was almost at hand.

THE DEAD AND THE DAMNED

After a long trek across the Hellwyrm Glacier, Settra's legions clashed with the warhost of Khagul Bloodfist – the last and most powerful of the Marauders and the one who had stolen Settra's crown all those years ago. In the intervening years, Khagul's victories had seen him become a mighty Champion of Chaos, imbued with the power of Dark Gods whose names men fear to speak. Khagul commanded a great horde of Chaos, for his fame was such that tribesmen and warbands from leagues around flocked to his blood-drenched banner. It was not only the Chaos Gods who had noticed the deeds of this warrior, for Prince Apophas, the Cursed Scarab Lord, saw in Khagul a soul that might be the equal of his own; a spirit that could buy his freedom from the tortures of the Nehekharan Underworld. So it was that whilst Settra led the fight against the assembled Chaos horde, carving his way through their armoured ranks, Apophas ambushed the unsuspecting Khagul.

The Chaos Champion had just finished dismembering a Tomb Scorpion when he was suddenly enveloped by a swarm of black beetles, which obscured his vision before coalescing

into a shape resembling that of a man. The figure clutched a dagger in one hand, and his leering skull seemed to stare into Khagul's very soul. Without pause, Khagul's bodyguard launched themselves at the assassin, but the figure opened its mouth and vomited forth a surge of insects that drowned them beneath chitinous bodies. Apophas stalked towards his target, and Khagul readied his axe. The Chaos Champion hacked at the figure with frenzied swipes, but it was to no avail. Every time Khagul cut into Apophas' body a tide of scuttling scarabs would flow over the wound. In frustration, he raised his axe high above his head, preparing to strike the assassin's skull from its shoulders but, before the stroke fell, Apophas had slashed his dagger across the champion's throat. Khagul's blood burst forth in an arterial spray, and he slumped to his knees. Apophas drew the warrior's soul from his mortal body, capturing it before dragging it into the Underworld for all eternity.

With the death of Khagul, the cohesion the Chaos warhost crumbled. The northern tribesmen reverted to their crude, berserk nature, and they were easily dashed against Settra's disciplined battle lines. The King of all Nehekhara smashed into the ranks of mortals time and again, leaving a trail of fire and death in his wake. Against this onslaught, the hearts of men faltered, and the barbaric tribesmen turned tail and fled, only to be run down by regiments of Undead cavalry that Settra had positioned for just such a task. Only the armoured warriors of the Chaos host stood their ground, and they fought against Khemri's war-statues in a clash of steel

and stone, but when Settra's chariot legions smashed into the Chaos Warriors' flanks, they too were massacred. It would be two more days before Settra's legions butchered the final remnants of the Chaos horde, the bloody campaign ending when Settra himself charged through a hailstorm to slay a lightning wreathed Shaggoth. The snow plains were littered with the bodies of dead, and from amidst the corpses Settra retrieved the bloodstained Crown of Nehekhara. Settra's treasures had finally been recovered, and those who had wronged him now lay dead at his feet. Such was the fate for any who dared oppose the will of Settra the Imperishable.

THE WRATH OF KING PHAR

King Phar of Numas arose from his sarcophagus angry that his slumber had been disturbed. However, when his Liche Priests informed him that tomb robbers had plundered his treasure vaults, his wrath found new focus. Furious at the desecration, King Phar summoned his army to war. He could sense that his treasure lay in distant lands, and the discovery of several Night Goblin corpses within the royal treasure vaults was all the proof he needed. With all due haste, the legions of King Phar filed out of his pyramid and headed into the Badlands.

Unbeknownst to King Phar, he was being manipulated by the schemes of Thanquol, a nefarious Skaven Grey Seer. The Skaven sorcerer had long been searching for a means of destroying the Orcs and Goblins that dwelt within the

Dragonback Mountains – the formidable Blackclaw tribe. Despite several Skaven assaults, Thanquol could not oust the greenskins from their fortress-lair or get at the warpstone meteorites rumoured to have crashed into the mountain the previous year. Instead of risking his own life in another dangerous assault, Thanquol devised a plot whereby another would battle with the Orcs on his behalf – the dread legions of the Tomb Kings. Thanquol only needed to lure the dead man-things to the Dragonback Mountains, which he did by hiring Clan Eshin agents to infiltrate the pyramid of the ancient dead and steal numerous talismans and amulets. The shadowy agents left evidence of the Blackclaw tribe within the pyramid, and in the dead of night they planted the stolen treasure about their greenskin scapegoats.

ASSAULT ON THE BADLANDS

The legions of King Phar stood arrayed before the Orc stronghold of Dragonback Mountain, regiments of Skeletons standing perfectly still in serried ranks as they awaited their Tomb King's command. Above the sea of bone, golden banners glinted in the sunlight and ragged papyrus scrolls fluttered in the unearthly breeze as the air itself warped and shifted with magical energy. King Phar stood unmoving upon his ornate war chariot. In the distance, the Tomb King heard the deep, heavy pounding of tribal drums alerting the Orcs to his army's approach. He had experienced that same sound many centuries ago when blood flowed within his mortal flesh. Back then, those same drumbeats had chilled him with the thought of the coming battle. Now he felt nothing but cold contempt for these pitiful creatures, and he would be glad to purge them from the face of the world.

The greenskins poured out from their ramshackle fortress. At first they seemed an undisciplined horde, but the Tomb King knew better than to underestimate their instinctive warlike abilities. Within minutes, a solid wall of greenskins faced his army and advanced forwards. The Tomb King turned his crowned skeletal head towards his Skeleton Archers. Raising his golden-edged sword, he signalled them to loose their arrows skyward. Before the first cloud of arrows had descended into the ranks of the Orcs and Goblins, a second volley was airborne. King Phar watched with satisfaction as arrows that appeared to be sailing over the heads of the enemy twisted in mid-flight, careening down into the centre of the greenskins' formations. Hundreds fell with the first volley, followed by more seconds later. Then King Phar's catapults fired, and the sky was ablaze with screaming skulls. These terrifying missiles smashed into the savage horde with horrific effect, felling even the mighty Trolls that lumbered beside their greenskin masters. Within minutes, the solid wall of Orcs and Goblins was in disarray, and they began to flee back towards their keep. It appeared as though they had been defeated.

Then, bursting from the gates, there rode a mighty Orc Warboss. Mounted on a huge boar and clad in crude iron armour, he bawled at the panic-stricken Orcs, who then turned to face the Tomb King's army. Phar signalled to his troops again, and regiments of Skeleton Warriors closed ranks into perfectly formed defensive blocks, the sun shining off many thousands of bronze spear points.

Following King Phar's lead, the phalanxes of his army marched as one towards the brutish, braying hordes. The

Orcs smashed into the Skeleton Warrior's shield wall with ferocious force, yet the undying soldiers did not take a single step back. Uttering ancient incantations, King Phar's Liche Priests replenished the ranks of the fallen, and slowly but surely the legions of Nehekhara began to cut the savage hordes down. Where the imposing Ushabti fought, scores of greenskins were hewn, but these formidable statues were soon shattered by green bolts of Orcish sorcery. Uttering an ancient curse, King Phar was more than satisfied to see the ground around the Shaman crack and split as a fearsome Tomb Scorpion rose from out of the earth. Its massive pincers sliced the Orc Shaman in half before its immense stinger thrust forwards, repeatedly striking a gaggle of smaller Goblin wizards who fell to the ground, convulsing as the liquefying poison took hold.

At an unseen command, the dusty ground to the Orcs' right flank burst open in a fountain of soil as dozens of Necropolis Knights emerged from the barren earth. They charged into the surprised Orcs and laid into their foe with merciless efficiency. At the very instant that the serpentine cavalry appeared, the skeletal battle line parted as King Phar led his chariot legions into the fray. The rumble of wheels and clatter of skeletal hooves sounded across the battlefield. Many hundreds of the gilded constructions smashed into the ranks of the greenskins, gold-trimmed wheels crushing untold numbers of Orcs and Goblins beneath them. Greenskins fled before the combined onslaught, and spears thrust through their unprotected backs. Phar's chariot rolled over several bodies before smashing into the Orc Warboss's boar riders, who had been taken by surprise by the severity of the charge. King Phar steered his chariot towards the massive Warboss and swung his blade in a wide arc. With a terrifying display of strength he cut the Orc in twain. Seeing the two halves of their chieftain fall away was more than the greenskins could take and, as their courage failed them, the brutes fled to the safety of the mountains.

As his warriors reclaimed golden artefacts from the slain, King Phar surveyed the corpse-strewn land around him. During his mortal reign he had cleared much of this mountainous region of Orc tribes. The time would come when he would conquer these lands again, but for now he wished only to return his treasures to their alcoves in Numas.

AMBUSH AT THE SALT PLAINS

King Phar's legions had not escaped the fighting unscathed, however. Having observed the battle, Thanquol reasoned they would be easier pickings and saw no reason why he should have to give up the bejewelled riches his agents had stolen after all. As King Phar returned to Numas, his forces were ambushed by the Grey Seer's army. The Skaven lay amongst the many temple ruins that littered the Salt Plains to the north of Numas, and when the unsuspecting regiments of King Phar's army entered range, they unleashed their infernal machines of war.

Arcs of warp lightning smashed apart dozens of golden chariots, and eldritch flames consumed whole regiments of Tomb Guard, their embalmed bodies set ablaze like tinder. Doomwheels trampled over the Tomb King's forces, crushing swathes of Skeletons to powdered bone as hundreds of mutated warbeasts rampaged into the Undead battlelines. Such an attack would have left mortal opponents

stunned and demoralised, but the soldiers of King Phar's legions no longer knew of such concepts, and silently they reformed their ranks to face this threat. However, the Skaven war machines were but a prelude to the full brunt of the attack, for countless thousands of Skaven warriors boiled out of the darkness, a black tide of mangy fur and rusty blades that spilled over the bone-dry land. From Phar's commanding viewpoint, the neat and disciplined ranks of his own army were dwarfed by the teeming horde. Grey Seer Thanquol, leading from the back as any Skaven leader should, viewed the same scene from atop a shattered temple complex and rubbed his claws in glee; soon his enemies would be destroyed.

Lost in his dreams of triumph, Thanquol did not at first notice when the sky began to darken, for a great cloud of dust and sand seeped over the horizon. Only when a black, vulture-like shadow passed overhead, and vengeful spirits could be heard shrieking in the wind, did the Grey Seer pause to look behind him. Despite the searing heat of the desert day, what he saw made his blood run cold as ice. A second army of Skeletons had strode out of Numas, and the ancient incantations of the Liche Priests had lent their bleached limbs an unnatural swiftness. Phalanxes of Skeletons surged forwards as fast as the desert wind. However, it was the towering statues that advanced in their wake that truly terrified Thanquol; he saw a dozen Khemrian Warsphinxes striding abreast through the rising dust clouds. At the centre of this approaching army, standing atop a magnificent gilded Warsphinx, rode the regal form of Lamhirakh, son of King Phar and Tomb Prince of Numas, who had arrived to complete his father's trap.

King Phar was ancient beyond counting, and though wrathful that his sacred treasures had been plundered, he realised that the greenskins were not responsible. The Tomb King knew that Orcs and Goblins had little interest in golden talismans, especially not when there was an array of heavy bladed swords and mighty golden flails to steal instead. Now that the Skaven, the true thieves, had revealed themselves, he would see to their punishment.

THE TRAP IS SPRUNG

Having distracted the ratmen long enough, King Phar nodded to his Tomb Herald, standing as ever by his side. The deathless champion raised an elaborate standard, set with gilded skulls amidst a bedrock of blood-rubies, high into the sky before striking the ground with its golden haft. Magical light flashed from the point of impact, and thunder rumbled across the skies. For a moment, all was obscured by a howling whirlwind of sand, but when the dust settled, innumerable Skeleton Warriors had dragged themselves from their sandy graves below, answering the summons to fight beside their king once more. With his forces replenished, King Phar advanced into the tumult of the combat in front of him, driving his enchanted blade deep into the flesh of any living thing that stood in his way.

The musk of fear hung heavy around the Skaven as the two Undead forces closed about them. King Phar's forces relentlessly drove the hordes towards the Khemrian Warsphinxes. The ratmen crashed against the towering statues like a black sea against indomitable cliffs and they died in droves. A Doomwheel careened around and charged

the first of the gigantic constructs, but the stone edifice smashed the infernal contraption into matchwood beneath its heavy claws. Hundreds of Skaven were burned alive as the leonine statues roared, belching forth cones of flame; rat-blood stained the Salt Plains as the Undead crew brought their weapons down in sweeping arcs. Caught between the two armies, the Skaven were methodically butchered.

Panicked and desperate, Thanquol played his final gambit. Even as the Khemrian Warsphinxes pummelled the Skaven hordes underfoot, a single black-robed figure leapt out of the verminous sea and darted up the stone flanks of the golden monster at the formation's lead. Before any could react, a Skaven Assassin plunged a warpstone-poisoned dagger into Prince Lamhirakh's throat. No sooner had the ancient prince been killed than the assassin yelped in agony as a terrible curse wracked his body and his blood turned to sand in his veins. Though the destruction of Prince Lamhirakh did little to halt the advance of the Skeleton regiments, it allowed Thanquol the time he needed to escape and flee. The rest of his minions were not as quick, nor as fortunate.

Slowly, but inexorably, the two jaws of King Phar's legions clamped shut. The Liche Priests called upon the power of ancient gods, and magical light shone from the Skeleton Warriors' empty eye sockets as they cut their fear-stricken foes down with supernatural vigour. With the last Skaven slain by his own hands, King Phar returned to Numas content that the vile ratmen would think long and hard before disturbing his slumber again.

THE LEGIONS OF THE TOMB KINGS

The ancient armies of the Tomb Kings are vast beyond counting. Loyal even in death, legions of skeletal infantry, cavalry and chariots advance at the side of their mummified lords as a diverse array of giant stone effigies stride across the battlefield to smash their foes asunder. With such armies, the Tomb Kings crush their enemies and conquer whole kingdoms.

In this section, you will find details for all the different troops, heroes, monsters and war machines used in a Tomb Kings army. It provides the descriptions, imagery, characteristics profiles and special rules necessary to use all the elements of the Tomb Kings army, from Core Units to Special Characters, and from magic weapons to the arcane Lore of Nehekhara.

ARMY SPECIAL RULES

This section of the book describes all the different units used in a Tomb Kings army, along with the rules necessary to use them in your games of Warhammer. Where a model has a special rule that is explained in the Warhammer rulebook, only the name of that rule is given. If a model has a special rule that is unique to it, that rule is detailed alongside its description. However, there are a number of commonly recurring 'army special rules' that apply to several Tomb Kings units, and these are detailed below.

NEHEKHARAN UNDEAD

The Undead warriors of the Tomb Kings are no longer beings of flesh and blood, but sun-bleached bones animated by ritualistic magic. These fearless troops are petrifying to behold as they stride inexorably forwards to strike down the enemies of their Tomb King.

All units with the Nehekharan Undead special rule are Unbreakable, Unstable and cause Fear, as described in the Warhammer rulebook. In addition, units with the Nehekharan Undead rule can never (ever!) make march moves and, when charged, can only elect to hold.

THE HIEROPHANT

Hierophant is the title used to describe the army's highest-ranking Liche Priest. The army's Hierophant is responsible for awakening the Tomb King's legions from their ancient slumber. Without his magic, the spirits of the these warriors will be dragged back to the Realm of Souls.

Your army must include at least one Nehekharan Undead Wizard to be the army's Hierophant. If your army includes several Wizards, this will be the one with the highest Wizard Level. If two or more models have the highest Wizard Level, choose which of them will be the Hierophant. Remember to tell your opponent which one is the Hierophant at the start of the battle. The Hierophant must use the Lore of Nehekhara (see page 61).

The Hierophant uses his powers to bind the souls of the dead to the mortal realm and restore the bodies of fallen warriors. The Hierophant, and all models in the same unit, have the Regeneration (6+) special rule.

If the Hierophant is destroyed, the magical animus of the army starts to dissipate. At the end of the phase in which the Hierophant is removed as a casualty, and at the start of every friendly turn thereafter, all friendly Nehekharan Undead units on the battlefield must take a Leadership test. If the test is failed, the unit immediately suffers a number of Wounds equal to the amount by which it failed the Leadership test, with no saves of any kind allowed.

Example: The army's Hierophant is destroyed in the enemy's Shooting phase. At the end of the phase a unit of Skeleton Warriors (Ld 5) takes a Leadership test and rolls a 7. They therefore suffer two Wounds. At the beginning of the Skeleton Warriors' next turn, they take another Leadership test, and this time they roll a 6, resulting in a further Wound.

TOMB KINGS BATTLE STANDARD BEARER

The Tomb King's personal banner is inscribed with incantations that focus the magic binding his army together.

In addition to the normal rules for the army battle standard, units of Nehekharan Undead within 12" of their battle standard suffer one less Wound than they normally would due to the Unstable special rule, or following the death of the army's Hierophant.

ANIMATED CONSTRUCT

Alongside the skeletal legions stride statues of unyielding stone awakened by the most powerful of incantations.

All units with the Animated Construct special rule have an armour save of 5+. In addition, these units suffer one less Wound than they normally would as a result of the Unstable special rule, or following the death of the army's Hierophant. If a unit with the Animated Construct special rule is within 12" of the Battle Standard Bearer they will, therefore, suffer two less Wounds than they normally would.

ARROWS OF ASAPH

These arrows carry the blessing of the goddess Asaph, and they seek out their enemies with unerring accuracy.

Units with the Arrows of Asaph special rule never count any bonuses or penalties to hit when shooting, regardless of the source of the modifier.

RESURRECTING FALLEN WARRIORS

Some magic spells and items can restore lost Wounds and even resurrect fallen warriors in a Nehekharan Undead unit. Wounds regained in this way follow a strict order. First, the unit champion is resurrected, and then the musician (standard bearers are never resurrected – if the bearer has been destroyed, the banner crumbles to dust), displacing rank-and-file models as required. Then rank-and-file models with multiple Wounds (including command figures) are healed to their starting value. Finally, any remaining Wounds resurrect rank-and-file models. In the case of multiple-Wound rank-and-file models, the first resurrected models must be fully healed before another can be resurrected, and so on. Resurrected models are added to the front rank until it reaches at least five models (or three models if the target unit is monstrous infantry, monstrous beasts, monstrous cavalry or chariots) – additional models can then be added to the front or rear rank. If the unit already has more than one rank, models can only be added to the rear rank. A unit cannot be taken beyond its starting size. Unless specifically stated otherwise, spells and magic items that restore lost Wounds cannot heal characters or their mounts. If a character has joined a unit, only the unit will recover lost Wounds.

ENTOMBED BENEATH THE SANDS

Many skeletal warriors and statues lie dormant beneath the baking sands of Nehekhara, awaiting the signal to burst through the desert surface and ambush their foes.

A unit with this ability has the Ambushers special rule, with the following exceptions. When these units enter the battle in the Remaining Moves sub-phase, they do not move onto the board as reinforcements in the normal way. Instead, when a unit that is Entombed Beneath the Sands enters the battle, place a small marker (such as a coin) anywhere on the battlefield, but not in impassable terrain or within 1" of a deployed unit. Roll a scatter dice and an artillery dice. If you roll a Hit on the scatter dice, the marker stays in place. If you roll an arrow, move the marker the number, in inches, indicated by the artillery dice in the direction shown. If the marker is under a unit (friend or foe), impassable terrain or a building, place it 1" away from the closest edge of the unit/terrain. Once the final position of the marker is established, place the emerging unit in a legal formation such that it touches the marker, facing any direction. If you roll a misfire, or if for any reason some of the models in the unit cannot be placed, then the unit does not emerge. Instead, remove the marker and roll on the Mishap table. If a unit emerges successfully, it may act normally this turn (remember that, as it is the Remaining Moves sub-phase, the unit cannot declare a charge). Only characters that have the Entombed Beneath the Sands special rule can be deployed within such units. If you have several units Entombed Beneath the Sands, then repeat this process, one unit at a time.

ENTOMBED BENEATH THE SANDS MISHAP TABLE

1-2 Reclaimed by the Desert

The spirits animating the Undead are drawn back to the Realm of Souls before they can claw their way to the surface.

The entire unit is destroyed and treated as casualties.

3-4 Buried Too Deep

Buried far deeper than expected beneath the surface, the warriors fail to emerge in time to ambush their foes.

The unit is delayed and does not emerge – but you'll be able to try again next turn to see if it arrives, following the same process.

5-6 Shifting Sands

The entombed warriors emerge, but the shifting sands of Nehekhara have swept them away from their expected position.

The unit enters the battlefield from any point on a randomly determined board edge, moving on using the rules for reinforcements.

TOMB KINGS

Tomb Kings are the ancient, long-dead rulers of Nehekhara. Their mummified corpses have been awakened by magical incantations, and their bodies are now inhabited by their undying, vengeful spirits. The Tomb Kings have been reborn to a mocking imitation of life, transformed into hideous cadavers whose kingdoms have been plundered and lost. Bitter and twisted, the Tomb Kings' rage fuels an unremitting need to conquer; they are the true monarchs of the dead, and they are coming to reclaim their rightful dominion.

Upon their first death, the Tomb Kings were embalmed in elaborate ceremonies. Their bodies were wrapped in pitch-soaked bandages inscribed with magical wards meant to preserve their corpses for all eternity. Despite the skills of the Liche Priests, the Tomb Kings now resemble dried skeletal husks. They are, however, possessed of an incredible strength and can withstand injuries that would slay a mortal man outright. The only known way to truly destroy a Tomb King is to set their bone-dry forms ablaze.

Revived by the rituals of the Liche Priests, a Tomb King awakens from the sleep of death possessing all the ambition and lust for power he had in life. Every Tomb King seeks to reclaim his plundered treasures and restore his ancient glory. If this means the subjugation and destruction of foreign lands, then the Tomb King's army, loyal even in death, rises

from its rest at his command. Although it is the magic of the Liche Priests that animates the Tomb King's army, it is by the indomitable will of the Tomb King himself that they move and fight. Every Tomb King is an aggressive warlord, able to instil their warriors with their own unyielding vigour.

A powerful curse hangs over the mummified royalty of Nehekhara, striking down those who seek to do them wrong. Tales abound of tomb robbers dropping dead as their blood magically turns into sand or they are engulfed in a ravenous swarm of desert locusts that strip flesh from bone. The most horrible fates are reserved for those that dare strike down these ancient lords in combat – those who would willingly, and foolishly, bring about such a demise are truly damned.

TOMB PRINCES

Tomb Princes are the sons of the Tomb Kings. Each of the kings of ancient Nehekhara had many heirs, doubtless the result of their extensive harems, but only one could succeed their father to the throne. This was typically the second son of the king, for the firstborn were given to the gods to serve in the Mortuary Cult. The king's younger sons served as the generals and lieutenants of his armies and enforced his will over his subjects. Upon their deaths they were entombed beside the great tomb chamber of their sovereign, in an eternal council of war, waiting for the moment of awakening when they shall resume command of their Undead legions.

	M	WS	BS	S	T	W	I	A	LD
Tomb King	4	6	3	5	5	4	3	4	10
Tomb Prince	4	5	3	4	5	3	3	3	9

TROOP TYPE: Infantry (Character).

SPECIAL RULES: Flammable, Nehekharan Undead.

The Curse: If a model with the Curse rule is removed from play, then the enemy unit responsible – by inflicting the final wound, for example – will immediately suffer D6 Strength 5 hits (if the model was a Tomb King) or D6 Strength 4 hits (if the model was a Tomb Prince). These Wounds are distributed as for shooting hits. In close combat, any Wounds inflicted count towards the combat result. If more than one unit is responsible for the destruction of the model with the Curse (it is destroyed by the combat result in a multiple combat due to its Unstable rule, for example), then all guilty units are affected. If the model is killed in a challenge, then only his opponent is cursed, and not the whole enemy unit.

My Will Be Done: Any unit of Nehekharan Undead accompanied by a model with this rule uses the character's unmodified Weapon Skill in place of its own (use the highest Weapon Skill if the unit is joined by several characters with this rule). If all characters with the My Will Be Done rule in the unit are killed, the unit immediately reverts to using its own Weapon Skill. This special rule has no effect on mounts or any other characters – these always use their own Weapon Skill.

LICHE PRIESTS

Liche Priests are the undying members of Nehekhara's Mortuary Cult, and they hold the secrets to unlife. They know the rituals needed to draw forth spirits from the Realm of Souls and bind them once more into corporeal bodies. It is the Liche Priests who rouse the Tomb Kings and their courts from their slumber and awaken their armies for war. Liche Priests are also the keepers of Nehekhara's arcane lore. Through ritualistic incantations, they call upon the power of ancient gods to bestow blessings upon the warriors of the Tomb Kings, infusing their ancient bones with magical energy. Similarly, Liche Priests cast terrible curses upon their foes, summoning vengeful desert spirits to feast on their souls.

Since its founding, the Mortuary Cult was commanded to study the arts of mummification and communion with the gods. Steadily, over many centuries, the priests learned how to preserve a corpse from decay until the art of embalming had become very elaborate. The priesthood also devised a vast lore of magical incantations and rituals intended to bind the souls of the dead kings back into their royal bodies. Since a king depended on the Mortuary Cult's knowledge and loyalty in order to live beyond his own death, the Liche Priests held great power in ancient Nehekhara. Indeed, Liche Priests were the only subjects who could not be executed. In this way, the priesthood became a formidable power behind many thrones. Liche Priests acted as advisors and viziers to the kings of Nehekhara, and their status was second only to that of the ruling families.

Each necropolis, with the burial pyramids of the Tomb Kings at its core, has a temple dedicated to Nehekhara's Mortuary Cult, and it is here where the Liche Priests preside. In addition to the rituals of summoning, Liche Priests have many duties to perform in the necropolis, including renewing the seals upon the portals of the tomb vaults, maintaining the incantations of preservation, and determining the moment of a Tomb King's awakening. The Liche Priests continue to perform these duties for centuries because they cannot die a natural death, cursed forever by their own lust for immortality.

Long ago, the Liche Priests used their accumulated knowledge to trap their own souls within their bodies, and in doing so they extended their lives far beyond those of mortal men. However, whilst their spirits never passed into the Realm of Souls, their bodies have withered with the passing of centuries, and it is their spirit alone that now animates their forms. Without realising it, the entire priesthood cursed itself – not to eternal life, but to eternal undeath. Liche Priests' physical bodies are now little more than withered corpses. Hunched and frail, their dry, wizened skins are stretched like old parchment over their brittle skeletons. Each is garbed in an elaborate headdress, and clutched in their skeletal hands are ritual knives and rune-inscribed staffs, which act as both the Liche Priests' crutches and symbols of office.

The Liche Priests believe the Winds of Magic to be the breath of their gods, a power that connects the mortal world to the realms beyond. The magical incantations of

Nehekhara's Liche Priests have been perfected over millennia, and they have remained unchanged since that time. The wording of each and every incantation is recorded on dusty papyrus scrolls written in the mysterious hieroglyphs of Nehekhara's ancient language. Uttered in long, monotonous rituals, the incantations of the Liche Priests must be precisely pronounced, for the slightest mistake can incite the wrath of the gods. It is not unknown for the angered deities to snap the bones of the offending Liche Priest, set his form ablaze or even rend his soul asunder as punishment – such are the risks when harnessing the power of gods.

	M	WS	BS	S	T	W	I	A	LD
Liche High Priest	4	3	3	3	4	3	2	1	8
Liche Priest	4	3	3	3	3	2	2	1	7

TROOP TYPE: Infantry (Character).

MAGIC: Liche Priests are Wizards, and use spells from one of the following: the Lore of Nehekhara (see page 61), the Lore of Light or the Lore of Death.

SPECIAL RULES: Nehekharan Undead.

TOMB HERALDS

A Tomb Herald is the personal champion and trusted bodyguard of a Tomb King. Obedient to a fault, these mummified warriors cut down their lord's enemies without pause or hesitation, slicing through flesh and bone with every strike until all their foes lie dead or dying at their feet.

Tomb Heralds were selected from the ranks of the elite Tomb Guard, devout warriors who had honed their skills through years of warfare. Every candidate for the rank of Tomb Herald first had to pass numerous trials of bravery and loyalty to prove worthy of the honour.

Anyone wishing to harm a Tomb King must first get past his Herald, a sworn bodyguard who moves to intercept a mortal blow, heedless of the danger. A Tomb Herald was not just a bodyguard, but also a soul-guard – his life was intrinsically bound to that of his charge, for upon his king's death he was expected to slit his own throat and serve his monarch in the Realm of Souls. A Tomb Herald was then embalmed and buried at the right-hand side of his lord in order to watch over and protect the king's spirit for all eternity. A Tomb Herald's golden armour was placed over his death shrouding and his enchanted blade placed in his hand. Thus, when the Tomb King awakens from his sarcophagus, his most loyal retainer is already standing at his side, ready to slay his liege-lord's foes and enforce his will over the lands once more.

A Tomb Herald had many duties aside from the protection of his king. Disputes between Tomb Kings of different cities would be settled by a ritual duel between their nominated champions, and the Tomb Heralds often fulfilled this role. Sometimes these battles were fought to first blood, but such were the Tomb Heralds' skills in the art of slaughter that the first blow struck was often a killing strike. A Tomb Herald was also the envoy and harbinger of his Tomb King. Only when given the duty of bearing their lord's commands to distant parts of the realm would a Tomb Herald leave his charge's side, but when they did, they were empowered to speak with the king's voice. Thus, to disobey the orders of a Tomb Herald was treason, and was met with death at the champion's own ruthless hands.

The king's personal icon is often carried into battle by his Tomb Herald. This honour is reserved for only the most trusted of warriors, for each banner is a priceless heirloom. These lavish standards were crafted by master artisans, encrusted with a fortune of jewels and inlaid with finely lacquered wood, gold and lapis lazuli. Emblazoned upon their imposing surfaces are images of death and immortality, and pennants declaring the king's conquests hang below them. The passing of centuries has not tarnished the magnificence of these icons, and they are held as high as they were in ancient times, proudly announcing the deathly majesty of the Tomb King and his eternal army. However, the Tomb King's personal icon is not only a symbol of his wealth and power; they were also magical relics infused with powerful incantations meant to preserve and protect his legions in the next life. It was even said that the breath of Nehekhara's gods touched these icons, blessing them with a portion of their power. The king's most trusted warrior thus protected these artefacts, for superstition had it that if they fell in battle, the gods themselves would curse the king for all eternity.

	M	WS	BS	S	T	W	I	A	LD
Tomb Herald	4	4	3	4	4	2	3	3	8

TROOP TYPE: Infantry (Character).

SPECIAL RULES: Flammable, Killing Blow, Nehekharan Undead.

Sworn Bodyguard: If you have any Tomb Kings or Tomb Princes in your army, you must nominate one of them for the Tomb Herald to protect at the start of the game. The same character may not be nominated by several Tomb Heralds – the oath is a sacred one between a master and his chosen champion. Whenever the nominated character suffers a Wound (before saves are taken) and the Tomb Herald is in the same unit as him, roll a D6. On a 1, the Wound is resolved as normal, but on a 2+ the Wound is intercepted, and re-allocated to the Tomb Herald. No more than one Wound can be re-allocated to each Tomb Herald in each phase. Wounds suffered by a Tomb King or Prince in a challenge can't be re-allocated – it is a duel of honour, and the Tomb Herald may not intefere.

NECROTECTS

Necrotects were the artisans of ancient Nehekhara. They were not common labourers, but architects of extraordinary skill whose ambitions far outpaced what could be achieved in a mortal lifespan. In death, the Necrotects have lost none of their frenetic drive. They are filled with a compulsive need to pull down the inferior, vulgar cities of their enemies and supplant them with vast monuments of their own design.

The skills of a Necrotect were in high demand, for every king needed monuments to pronounce his majesty and a vast tomb to house his mortal remains upon his death. Indeed, Necrotects were so valued that, upon completing their work, they were rewarded with a ritual execution followed by an elaborate embalming ceremony. Many Necrotects were entombed within the same pyramids they had built, buried with the tools of their trade and an intricately carved death mask made by their own hands. The reasoning behind their sacrifice was twofold. Firstly, the king would need artisans to fashion palaces of gold in the next life. Secondly, it ensured that no rival kings could hire their services to commission a more elaborate tomb for themselves. Many Necrotects went to their graves willingly, perhaps for the honour of their beloved king, or because they were unable to live knowing that nothing they created would ever surpass their lord's tomb. Other Necrotects, particularly those whose creative desires still burned strongly, tended to meet with unfortunate accidents such as falling through rotten scaffolding, tripping on slippery stairwells, or drinking poisoned wine.

Necrotects were stern taskmasters who oversaw tens of thousands of Nehekharans as they toiled under the blazing sun. Under their gaze, an army of masons carved huge slabs of rock out of cliff faces before vast columns of slaves dragged the stones across the desert and hauled them into position. All Necrotects were foul tempered, and they would dispense summary punishment at the slightest provocation. They hated anything and anyone that threatened their art. In death, much of their work lies broken or damaged by the greed of tomb robbers and invading armies. Necrotects have been driven to a blinding rage by the wanton desecration of their beloved masterpieces, and they have sworn to have revenge. In battle, Necrotects lead the Tomb King's regiments like the work gangs of old. They exude the same aura of hatred they possessed in life, and their mere presence instils a magical state of fury in the Undead warriors of Nehekhara. Necrotects no longer need to extort their followers to work faster, and they reserve the lash for those who would defile their art instead, attacking these ignorant wretches with the crack of a whip strong enough to split open backs and leave spines exposed to the elements.

Necrotects saw to the fine details of construction personally, for only they possessed the skills necessary to carve the likeness of the gods into their sculptures and engrave intricate hieroglyphs onto their surfaces. These were not merely ornamental, for the Necrotects were schooled by the Liche Priests in the ways of crafting potent symbols of preservation. Necrotects may not know the full range of the Liche Priests' incantations, but they could inscribe powerful wards nonetheless. In unlife, Necrotects constantly repair their work, for many hieroglyphs have faded through the passage of time. When a Tomb King awakens, the Necrotects redouble their efforts as they attempt to finish their work. They tirelessly restore the great war-statues that stride to battle alongside the Tomb King's skeletal legions, renewing the hieroglyphs of protection. In battle, as Necrotects chant sinister mantras, these inscriptions glow, and the cracked stone of these animated statues flows to repair itself.

	M	WS	BS	S	T	W	I	A	LD
Necrotect	4	3	3	4	4	2	3	2	7

TROOP TYPE: Infantry (Character).

SPECIAL RULES: Flammable, Hatred, Nehekharan Undead.

Wrath of the Creator: The Necrotect confers the Hatred special rule onto his unit. If he leaves the unit, or is slain, the unit immediately loses Hatred.

Stone Shaper: Any unit of Animated Constructs within 12" of a character with the Stone Shaper rule gains the Regeneration (6+) special rule.

SKELETON WARRIORS

As the punishing midday sun blazes, the sands begin to shift, and thousands of sun-bleached skulls pierce the endless tracts of desert – sand pouring out through empty eye sockets as the Undead break the surface. Rising up from the dusty dunes come the eternal legions of the Tomb Kings; rank upon rank of Skeleton Warriors ready to kill once more in the name of their immortal monarchs. Holding curved swords and long spears, ancient forms awake from their deathly slumbers, forming up into vast regiments with a supernatural discipline that few living warriors can hope to match.

The mighty armies of Nehekhara, made up of regiment after regiment of valiant soldiers, swore oaths of eternal loyalty before the gods to serve their monarch in life and beyond into death. Thus, the bones of those who perished in battle were collected from the field of war and interred in the great tomb pits of their king's necropolis by the Liche Priests. Soldiers

who yet lived after their liege lord had died marched on, as if in a victory parade, to the necropolis on the day of the king's entombment. They strode into cavernous vaults and mighty walled courtyards, their Master of Arms leading from the front. Here they stood in regiments with their full paraphernalia of war, everything that would be needed to serve in the king's eternal army. Arranged in ranks, icons held proudly, the legions were entombed alive. No soldier flinched as the great stones were heaved into position, blocking out the light of the sun. Bravely, these warriors stood to attention as hot sand was poured into the tomb pits until the tops of standard poles disappeared from sight. There they remained until summoned by the incantations of the Liche Priests to heed the will of their king once more.

The Skeleton Warriors of Nehekhara are not mindless automatons slaved to the will of an evil necromancer. They are instead animated by the souls of their former bodies. The incantations of the Liche Priests summon the spirits of long-dead soldiers from the Realm of Souls and bind them into corporeal forms. However, without the extensive mummification lavished upon their lords and betters, the spirits of these warriors do not retain the full memory of their former existence. Upon awakening from their death-sleep, the only things that every one of these Undead soldiers can recall with perfect clarity is their unswerving loyalty to their king and the ways of war that were drilled into them in life. Thus, the skeletal regiments of Nehekhara obey every command of their Tomb King without hesitation – as they served him in life, so they serve him in death.

The Skeleton Warriors of Nehekhara are the backbone of a Tomb King's army. Under the shadow of gold-topped banners, vast phalanxes of skeletal troops advance in perfect unison towards the enemy, their polished weapons dazzling in the desert sun. As one, the skeletal soldiers turn and raise their large shields, presenting a hedge of deadly spear points to their foes. At an unseen command the Undead advance, wordlessly slaying those in their path without any thought of mercy. Skeletons are implacable warriors that know neither fear nor fatigue. Only a mortal who can overcome his fears and steady his trembling sword arm may land a blow that can destroy such unnatural creatures.

At battle's end, the Skeleton Warriors walk back, alongside their king, to their tomb pits. The only soldiers to break ranks are those that gather up the splintered bones of their former comrades, carrying the broken remains back to their tombs as the living might carry the bodies of fallen heroes. Upon their return, the Skeleton Warriors are once more buried until their sovereign has need of them again.

	M	WS	BS	S	T	W	I	A	LD
Skeleton Warrior	4	2	2	3	3	1	2	1	5
Master of Arms	4	2	2	3	3	1	2	2	5

TROOP TYPE: Infantry.

SPECIAL RULES: Nehekharan Undead.

SKELETON ARCHERS

The Skeleton Archers of Nehekhara nock and loose volleys of arrows as they advance towards their foe without ever breaking stride. Raising their bows as one, the archers fire, reaching into quivers for another arrow before the first salvo has even reached the zenith of its trajectory. These Undead archers unleash great clouds of death that darken the sky moments before falling amidst the ranks of the enemy. Riders are pitched from mounts, and swathes of enemy infantry fall dead as bronze tipped arrows rain down upon them and pierce their bodies.

The kings of ancient Nehekhara knew the importance of delivering death from afar, and all of them maintained legions of highly disciplined archers. Loyal soldiers for all eternity, Skeleton Archers continue to practice their ways of war as they did in centuries long past. Awakened from the tomb pits of their king's necropolis by the magical incantations of the Liche Priests, every Skeleton Archer arises with a bow still clutched in one hand and a quiver of arrows held in the other.

There was a strong tradition of archery in ancient Nehekhara, and hunting was a popular sport amongst young princes. However, upon reaching adulthood, a prince was expected to leave behind such pastimes and devote his life to ruling his people. It became tradition for a newly crowned

king to honour the greatest marksmen amongst his legions with his royal bow. This chosen warrior was bestowed the title of Master of Arrows, a position that held much prestige amongst the common soldiery. However, it was said that should the Master of Arrows miss his target the first time he fired the bow on the field of war, his life was forfeit – such was the punishment for betraying the king's trust.

Skeleton Archers are unencumbered by the large, heavy shields of the Tomb Kings' other legions, allowing them the freedom needed to fire their long, curved bows. This leaves them with little protection against the swords and axes of their enemies, but any foe wishing them harm must first cross the killing ground, weathering a hailstorm of lethal arrows every step of the way. Only the most heavily armoured of foes can withstand such withering salvos. Less protected targets may instead turn and flee from the onslaught, but once an enemy has entered the sights of Skeleton Archers, the Undead will not stop until their foes have been killed. Skeleton Archers will relentlessly pursue their opponents, for hundreds of leagues if needed, loosing a volley of arrows every time their retreating foes re-enter range. Whilst their enemies will grow weary, the Undead warriors no longer have such concerns and will only pause in their advance when the last of their quarry lies dead. Surrounded by the arrow-pierced bodies of their slain enemies, these Skeleton Archers will then stand perfectly still, awaiting the orders of their king. If that order is not forthcoming, they stand motionless and forgotten beneath the glare of the desert sun, until they are buried by the shifting desert sands.

	M	WS	BS	S	T	W	I	A	LD
Skeleton Warrior	4	2	2	3	3	1	2	1	5
Master of Arrows	4	2	3	3	3	1	2	1	5

TROOP TYPE: Infantry.

SPECIAL RULES:
Arrows of Asaph, Nehekharan Undead.

BLESSED ARROWS

Every arrow fired by the Skeleton Archers of Nehekhara has been blessed by Asaph, the goddess of vengeance and magic, so that they seek out their foes with unerring accuracy. When loosed, these arrows swerve in mid-air, darting towards their prey with the speed of a striking snake. The ritual bestowing each arrow with Asaph's blessing is long and arduous. The wooden shafts are inscribed with incantations using the claws of dune scorpions and the black feathers of desert vultures are used to fletch them. The most important part of the ritual is performed by chanting acolytes in the heart of Asaph's sacred temples, where bronze arrowheads are forged and cooled in the blood of a hundred sacrificed serpents.

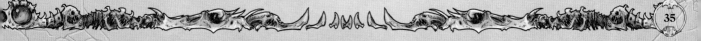

SKELETON HORSEMEN

Regiments of Skeleton Horsemen race across the sandy plains of Nehekhara mounted on the fleshless remains of their once-proud steeds, weapons lowered as they gallop towards their foes. These skeletal riders drive their heavy spears into their foes with bone-jarring force, using well-aimed thrusts that punch clean through torsos and rip open throats in a spray of blood. Those not impaled by the cavalry rider's razor-sharp spearheads are trampled into the ground by the thundering hooves of skeletal steeds.

Skeletal steeds instinctively obey the will of their riders, displaying the same supernatural discipline as the soldiery of the Tomb Kings' army. Only occasionally do these Undead horses twitch their heads as a vestigial memory of life surfaces. Even though their flesh has long since vanished, skeletal steeds are as powerful as they were in life, and they can crush a man's skull with a single kick.

Unencumbered by heavy armour or barding, a Tomb King's skeletal cavalry legions maintain a punishing pace as they traverse the scorching deserts of Nehekhara. Skeleton Horsemen often form the spearhead of a Tomb King's army and, as such, they are amongst the first of the Undead warriors to engage the foe. These vanguard warriors are not heavily armoured knights, but fearless raiders who launch devastating attacks where their opponents are weakest, luring the enemy into overextending their reach before withdrawing to strike again. However, Skeleton Horsemen are not completely without protection, for they carry large, sturdy shields in battle to deflect the panicked blows of their foes.

Cavalry were a relatively late addition to the armies of ancient Nehekhara, for horses needed a great deal of water to survive the desert heat. As such, steeds were expensive – worth considerably more than the soldiers who rode them. Only those warriors who had proven themselves, and slain a dozen foes in mortal combat, were inducted into the ranks of one of their king's valued cavalry legions. These warriors would then spend the rest of their lives fighting from the saddle, drilled under the tutelage of the king's Master of Horse – a grizzled veteran bearing the scars of several bloody campaigns. In life, these champions often formed part of the Tomb King's council of war, for their knowledge and experience of mounted warfare were second to none, and their expertise was highly valued.

When the Liche Priests summon the Tomb King's army from their sandy graves, fully formed cavalry columns stride out of the pyramids at the head of the foot legions. When the enemy is sighted, the cavalry regiment's hornblower signals the charge and a deep unsettling discord reverberates about the desert. This otherworldly sound shakes the dust from statues, and a disquieting feeling of dread permeates across the battlefield. As one, the Undead steeds gallop towards their quarry, the skeletal riders on their backs raising their shields and lowering their spears in perfect unison. Paralysed with fear, it is a brave foe indeed that does not flee as these deathless horsemen bear down upon them.

	M	WS	BS	S	T	W	I	A	LD
Skeleton Horseman	4	2	2	3	3	1	2	1	5
Master of Horse	4	2	2	3	3	1	2	2	5
Skeletal Steed	8	2	0	3	3	1	2	1	5

TROOP TYPE: Cavalry.

SPECIAL RULES: Nehekharan Undead, Vanguard.

AMANHOTEP THE INTOLERANT

During the time of the Desertblood Crusades, a regiment of Bretonnian Knights returned from Nehekhara with the remains of what they believed to be Duke Cheldric, a hero whose daring quest into the Land of the Dead was the stuff of legend. However, the Knights had actually returned to the Old World with the mummified body of King Amanhotep the Intolerant, who awakened after unknowingly being paraded up and down the length of Bretonnia and carried across a score of battlefields by zealous Battle Pilgrims. Amanhotep's wrath was great indeed, and he single-handedly slaughtered the inhabitants of dozens of towns before returning to his sarcophagus in Zandri.

SKELETON HORSE ARCHERS

The Skeleton Horse Archers of Nehekhara are likened to an angry desert wind, one that appears suddenly and leaves only the dead and the dying in its wake. Skeleton Horse Archers move relentlessly across the battlefield, firing volleys of magically blessed arrows into their foes before turning about and escaping retribution. As the Undead cavalry turn, they disappear from view as they ride into the cloud of dust thrown up by the hooves of their skeletal steeds. Before the cavalry archer's stunned victims can recover their wits, the Undead horsemen reappear, loosing another deadly salvo.

The horse archers of ancient Nehekhara were very different to the other living warriors in the king's army. They were not soldiers, raised and trained within the vast cities of Nehekhara, but nomadic tribesmen that dwelt in the deep desert. Such warriors knew the ways of the parched plains better than any city-born man, and with their swift mounts, they could traverse the shifting dunes without fear of getting lost. Such was their skill on horseback that they were said to have been born in the saddle and their marksmanship, unhindered by the jarring motion of their galloping mounts, was renowned throughout Nehekhara. The kings had great need of such warriors and guides, and they would pay much gold to hire their services as mercenaries. It was not until the reign of Rakaph III, of the second dynasty, that horse archers became a permanent feature in the armies of Nehekhara. Rakaph granted these tribes the freedom of the desert, the protection of his grand armies and as much gold as their chieftains could carry, in exchange for an annual tithe of warriors who would swear an oath of unswerving loyalty and obedience to the king. Ever since then, the kings of ancient Nehekhara maintained strong contingents of horse archers amongst their armies.

Skeleton Horse Archers are the outriders and scouts of the Tomb Kings army. Whereas mortal horses need regular rest and water, skeletal steeds cross the vast tracts of open desert at a relentless pace. Even in death, these Undead horsemen maintain an innate ability to track and hunt their quarry through the shifting dunes, and no sandstorm can obscure their targets from them. As scouts, Skeleton Horse Archers hinder the movements of the enemy and harass their flanks in fleeting, yet bloody skirmishes. These attacks do much to slow the advance of the Tomb King's enemies, pinning them in place while the Tomb King manoeuvres his own warriors into position.

When Skeleton Horse Archers attack, they strike without warning or mercy. The first an enemy soldier knows that he is in danger is when a black fletched arrow plunges into the throat of the man next to him, the gurgling cry of pain a ghastly prelude of the slaughter to come. An instant later another comrade falls to the ground, an arrow shaft protruding from his blood-slick chest as his pierced heart empties its contents onto the desert sands. With every passing second more arrows find their mark, falling amongst the enemy like a deadly rain. As the Skeleton Horse Archers close upon their foes, their enemy sees them for the first time, appearing through the haze of the desert heat like a terrifying mirage. At a silent command, the skeletal riders urge their Undead mounts forwards and the archers'

grinning skulls turn to face the panic-stricken survivors. With eyeless sockets never wavering from their targets, the Skeleton Horse Archers raise their weapons and draw back bowstrings once more. As mortal warriors turn and flee for their lives, the last thing they ever feel is the searing agony of an arrow slamming into their backs.

	M	WS	BS	S	T	W	I	A	LD
Skeleton Horseman	4	2	2	3	3	1	2	1	5
Master of Scouts	4	2	3	3	3	1	2	1	5
Skeletal Steed	8	2	0	3	3	1	2	1	5

TROOP TYPE: Cavalry.

SPECIAL RULES: Arrows of Asaph, Fast Cavalry, Nehekharan Undead, Scouts.

"Lightning will sunder the skies, the rivers will flow with blood and war will come to the land. The legions of the long-dead kings shall once more rise in eternal conquest, and death shall ride beside them."

– Settra, The Eternal King of Nehekhara.

SKELETON CHARIOTS

The pride of a Tomb King's army is his charioteer legions. Their advance is heralded by a cloud of dust thrown high into the air as they drive across the sands. Moments later, units of these deadly machines crest the dunes, their wheels whirring as they careen towards their foe. The legions impact with bone-shattering force, wave after wave of chariots crushing bodies beneath heavy wheels as their Undead crew lay about the disorientated foe with lethal effect.

Nehekhara was the first great civilisation of Mankind and the place where men first used horse and chariot in battle. This was a great accomplishment, for horses had only recently been bred as beasts of war, but it was considered undignified for those of noble blood to touch such lowly brutes, let alone ride them. However, with the invention of the chariot, the ruling classes of Nehekhara could take to battle with the speed of a stallion. The ancient armies of Nehekhara included vast forces of swift chariots and each carried an arsenal of weaponry. To fight from such an armoured platform was thought to be the height of civilised warfare. As such, only royalty and nobility were permitted to fight as charioteers. As befitted their status, charioteers were bedecked in fine armour, precious metals and valuable jewels. Their chariots were created by skilled artisans, often gilded in gold and covered with images of skulls, bones and other symbols of the Mortuary Cult.

The fighting quality of the king's charioteers was a reflection of his own power and martial prowess. As such, the king entrusted the training of these regiments to the Master of Chariots. These scarred warriors were typically a minor blood relation to the royal family, such as a cousin, and thus had the aristocratic superiority to back up his years of fighting experience. The Master of Chariots was a ruthless disciplinarian, and under his command, the noble-born charioteers were drilled until they were elite warriors fit to fight in the king's name. They would ride into battle fierce and proud, the legion's standard carried high as they bore down upon their foes.

Ever since their invention, chariots have been the chosen means of transport for the kings of Nehekhara. Upon awakening from their deathly slumbers, Tomb Kings have continued to lead their armies to war from atop these ancient machines. Not only does a chariot have an armoured carriage, to protect him from harm as he slays his foes with every sweep of his enchanted blade, it also provides him an elevated platform. This grants the Undead monarch a superior view of the battlefield, enabling a Tomb King to better witness the movements of enemy formations and direct his own troops to inflict the most damage.

Squadrons of chariots were entombed beside the pyramids of the Tomb Kings of Nehekhara, ready to serve their lords upon their awakening and trample over their enemies as they had done in his mortal reign. The mere sight of Skeleton Chariots arrayed for war and riding to battle is enough to strike fear in the hearts of all who oppose them. As the chariots rumble towards their quaking foe, slowly gathering speed until they are ready to charge, that fear turns to outright panic as the pride of Nehekhara crashes into them and the slaughter begins.

	M	WS	BS	S	T	W	I	A	LD
Skeleton Chariot	-	-	-	4	4	3	-	-	-
Skeleton Charioteer	-	3	2	3	-	-	2	2	7
Master of Chariots	-	3	2	3	-	-	2	3	7
Skeletal Steed	8	2	-	3	-	-	2	1	-

TROOP TYPE: Chariot (Armour Save 5+).

SPECIAL RULES:
Arrows of Asaph, Nehekharan Undead.

Chariot Legions: A rank of Skeleton Chariots only needs three models to count for rank bonus. In addition, Skeleton Chariots add their rank bonus to the Strength of any Impact Hits that they inflict.

'And the Tomb Kings Rode to War...': Characters in a Tomb Kings army that have a chariot (including Settra the Imperishable's Chariot of the Gods) can join a unit of Skeleton Chariots. They can remain with the unit even if their mount is destroyed but, if they subsequently leave the unit whilst on foot, they will not be able to rejoin it, or join another unit of Skeleton Chariots.

TOMB GUARD

The Tomb Guard are the partially mummified remains of the king's elite guard. They are exceptional warriors, maintaining all the discipline and martial skill they had in life. In battle, the Tomb Guard form unwavering ranks of armoured warriors. They have spilled the blood of their enemies for countless centuries, and numerous armies have been dashed against their implacable shield walls.

The bravest and best soldiers served as bodyguards for the ancient kings of Nehekhara. Elevation into the ranks of the Tomb Guard was perhaps the only way that a warrior not of noble-birth could ever hope to enter the royal palaces. The Tomb Guard lived in comparative luxury, each having a dozen slaves to tend to their wargear so they could keep their attentions focused on their sacred duties – the preservation of the king's life and dominion. However, worldly wealth was the least reward granted these warriors, for in respect of their position, they were honoured with the privilege of sharing his immortality. Upon their death, or that of their lord's, they were mummified by the Liche Priests and buried in close proximity to their king's sarcophagus. Just as they guarded the palace in life, so now they guard the inner sanctum of the necropolis in death. The prospect of sharing in the eternal beauty and immortality of their king, and serving him for all time, inspired these soldiers to heroic acts of bravery. They would die where they stood rather than

retreat and charge against the most hopeless odds without thought of their own survival. Time and again this selfless heroism would bring victory to the king's army and earn a place in his pyramid for the honoured fallen.

The Tomb Guard were entombed with their armour and weapons. Their bodies were further decorated with gold bracelets, headdresses and scarab-shaped brooches that fastened parchments proclaiming their deeds of bravery and devotion. The Tomb Guard rest, until awakened, in their stone sarcophagi, arranged upright around the royal tomb chamber of their king. Here they stand to attention as palace guards until the time comes when they are again needed. If intruders violate the tomb, they will awaken and defend their slumbering lord. If the king rouses from his death sleep, ready to go forth to conquer the lands of the living, they arise and form an honour guard at his side.

Although the Tomb Guard were rewarded with a form of mummification, the embalming rituals used were nowhere near as elaborate as the ceremonies that the Tomb Kings and Tomb Princes underwent. However, the Tomb Guard have been reborn with immortal bodies far stronger and more resilient than the flesh and blood forms they wore in life. Furthermore, Tomb Guard retain more of their former personalities than the massed soldiery of skeletal warriors. They awaken with memories of heroic deeds, bloody victories and the unyielding will to destroy their king's enemies still burning strongly in their minds. Above all they remember their duty to protect their Tomb King from harm, and any that threaten their charge are slain, cut down without pause.

As befits warriors of their standing, Tomb Guard were gifted with fine suits of leather armour and bronze scale studded with jewels and precious metals. They carry lavishly crafted shields, inlaid with skulls, bones and other symbols of death. In battle, the Tomb Guard wield weapons that have had powerful incantations of cursing imbued into them, with which they carve through the ranks of their enemy, cutting through necks and felling their foes with every blow.

	M	WS	BS	S	T	W	I	A	LD
Tomb Guard	4	3	3	4	4	1	3	1	8
Tomb Captain	4	3	3	4	4	1	3	2	8

TROOP TYPE: Infantry.

SPECIAL RULES:
Killing Blow, Nehekharan Undead.

"Sentinels at the portal of eternity, mighty ones who stand before the king, valiant heroes whom none shall pass, guardians of the king's tomb."

- Hieroglyphic inscription over the sarcophagi of Settra's Tomb Guard.

CASKETS OF SOULS

At the heart of each tomb of the mightiest kings there lies a casket, inscribed with hieroglyphs of malediction. Within this sarcophagus resides the tormented souls of those who have incited a Tomb King's wrath. Powerful binding inscriptions ensure that these souls cannot leave their prison until the moment when the casket is opened.

A Casket of Souls is not physically carried into battle, but is summoned through the incantations of a Keeper of the Casket – a priest of the Mortuary Cult whose sole responsibility is the custodianship of this revered object. As a Keeper of the Casket intones the proper chants, a fountain of skulls bursts from the ground below. These gush forth, forming into a mound that spills over revealing the Casket of Souls atop a dais of bone, with a nimbus of sorcerous energy swirling around its infernal form, and two Undead guardians by its side. The power surrounding the Casket of Souls is such that nearby Liche Priests can infuse their incantations with a portion of its energy.

When a Casket of Souls is opened, blinding light spills across the battlefield as countless souls scream into the air seeking freedom from the suffering of their confinement. These spirits plunge through the bodies of the Tomb Kings' enemies, and the hapless victims suffer unbearable agony as their life essence is utterly drained. To die thus is far worse than a physical death, for very the souls of those who perish in this manner become ensnared by the power of the casket. A Casket of Souls is a devastating weapon, for all who look upon it risk eternal damnation and imprisonment.

Only the attendant Keeper knows the incantations that will open the casket, and if he is interrupted the souls of the damned are instantly sucked back inside. If a Casket of Souls is ever destroyed, the tortured souls will escape their confines in a raging maelstrom of destruction, feeding on anything caught in the magical backlash as they wreak their vengeance.

	M	WS	BS	S	T	W	I	A	LD
Casket of Souls	-	-	-	-	10	3	-	-	-
Keeper of the Casket	4	3	3	3	3	1	3	2	8
Casket Guard	4	3	3	3	3	1	3	2	8

TROOP TYPE: War Machine.

Note: *The Casket of Souls model does not have a base – to determine its front arc, simply treat the model's square 'footprint', formed by the dais of bones, as though it were a standard base.*

SPECIAL RULES: **Killing Blow (Casket Guard only), Nehekharan Undead.**

Light of Death: *When the Casket of Souls opens, tortured spirits leap from foe to foe, leaving a trail of death in their wake.*

Innate bound spell (power level 5). The Casket of Souls can use this spell as long as the Keeper of the Casket model is alive, and the Casket of Souls has not moved this turn. *Light of Death* is a **direct damage** spell with a range of 48". The

target of *Light of Death* must take a Leadership test on 3D6, adding the results together. If the test is passed, nothing happens. Otherwise, for each point the unit failed the test by, it suffers an automatic Wound with no armour saves allowed, distributed as for shooting attacks.

Once the Leadership test has been resolved, roll a D6: on a 3 or more, choose another unengaged enemy unit within 6" of the initial target – the tortured souls leap to that unit, which must also suffer the effects of the *Light of Death* spell. Keep rolling for further victims (each within 6" of the last target struck), until the roll is failed or there are no more viable targets. A unit can only be the target of *Light of Death* once per Magic phase.

Covenant of Power: If you have one or more Caskets of Souls on the table at the start of your Magic phase, you add D3 power dice to your pool.

Unleashed Souls: If a Casket of Souls is destroyed, roll a D6 for every unit (friend or foe!) within 12" of the Casket before it is removed from play. On a roll of 4+, that unit immediately suffers D6 Strength 6 hits, distributed as for shooting. These are magical attacks, and no armour saves can be taken against them. After resolving the effects of Unleashed Souls, remove the Casket of Souls as normal.

SCREAMING SKULL CATAPULTS

The catapults of a Tomb King's eternal army are akin to the stone throwers of other races, but instead of flinging rocks at the foe, they throw volleys of flaming skulls. The Liche Priests cast terrible curses upon every one of these skulls, enchanting them so that they scream hideously as they are hurled through the air, rising to a deafening crescendo just before they strike their target. These are the very death screams of the skulls' former owners, the wailing shrieks of those slaughtered on the field of battle and the agonised cries of prisoners captured at the moment of their execution. Many battle-hardened warriors are driven to the edge of insanity by the blood-curdling sound. This horrific ammunition bursts into hellish, ethereal flames when it is launched, and as the skulls arc through the air, they blaze an eerie trail of green-fire behind them. Most of these skulls explode on impact, sending fragments of splintered bone in all directions and engulfing those nearby in a wash of balefire. Others smash into their target with horrifying force, infernal flames spilling out of empty eye sockets as the skulls chew through armour and warm flesh alike.

Every Screaming Skull Catapult is crewed by a trio of Skeleton Warriors. They load and fire their war machines with silent efficiency, unperturbed by the dreadful sound of their ammunition. The artisans of ancient Nehekhara wrought Screaming Skull Catapults into the very image of destruction. The catapults' arms were shaped to resemble twisted bones, and their cradles were fashioned into vast skeletal claws – the so-called hands of death. The chassis of the catapults were carved to resemble the skeletal remains of a vicious desert predator, and sprouting from their spines are great towers of skulls. These are the remains of enemy champions, nailed to the mast of the catapult as grisly trophies. There they wail in perpetual torment until plucked from their fastenings and fired at the enemy. Even the stoutest heart trembles with fear knowing that such a fate awaits them should they fall against the Tomb Kings.

King Behedesh of Zandri was the inventor of the Screaming Skull Catapult and he ordered many to be built during his reign. He used these extensively in many wars, and most famously to defeat the rulers of Araby who rebelled against him. These treacherous kings refused to submit to Behedesh's will, but when their armies were bombarded by the skulls of their own comrades, they fled and their cities burned. At every battle's end, the catapult crews scoured the battlefield for the bodies of slain foes, decapitating any they found and carrying the severed heads back to be cursed by Zandri's Liche Priests. However, such was not the fate for the rebel kings. Behedesh decreed that these traitors were to be mummified alive and strapped atop his catapults so that they could watch the destruction of their cities first hand. Even now, many centuries later, some catapults still have withered corpses bound to their timbers. Whether these are the same renegades that opposed Behedesh, or the remains of other tormented souls, has long been forgotten. Occasionally, a muffled sound, as faint as the rustling of dried parchment, ushers from their cadaverous lips, begging for mercy. However, the skeleton crews are oblivious to their pleas, and even if they were not, they could not be heard over the banshee wailing of their ensorcelled ammunition.

	M	WS	BS	S	T	W	I	A	LD
Screaming Skull Catapult	-	-	-	-	7	3	-	-	-
Skeleton Crew	4	2	2	3	3	1	2	1	5

TROOP TYPE: War Machine (Stone Thrower).

SPECIAL RULES: Nehekharan Undead.

Screaming Skulls: All shooting attacks made by a Screaming Skull Catapult are magical and have the Flaming Attacks special rule.

In addition, any unit that suffers one or more casualties from a shooting attack by a Screaming Skull Catapult must take a Panic test as if it had taken 25% casualties.

UPGRADES:

Skulls of the Foe: Some Screaming Skull Catapults fire the cursed skulls of fallen enemies, making the tormented screams of the grisly ammunition all the more terrifying.

This upgrade adds an additional effect to the catapult's Screaming Skulls. If a target unit takes a Panic test as a result of being hit by the Skulls of the Foe, then they must take the test with a -1 penalty to their Leadership.

CARRION

Carrion are giant Undead birds of prey that feast on the carcasses of the fallen. Their broad wings, covered in feathers as black as midnight, darken the sky and spread the shadow of doom upon those dying in the desert. Carrion can smell blood from leagues away, and they are drawn to battlefields like moths to flame. Wherever Carrion are seen to fly, death and carnage are surely nearby.

Carrion resemble the black desert vultures that inhabit the plains of Nehekhara, but they are far larger and more dangerous creatures. Carrion are repulsive scavengers that stand taller than a man and have vast wingspans. They have bodies that are decayed and bloated with death. Putrefied ropes of muscle hang from their frames as they fly with slow, sorrowful strokes of tattered wings. Bones poke through the rotten skin of Carrion, and gashes in their distended bellies often expose the skeletal contents of their last rotting meal. Carrion are bald headed creatures, and in life they would push their long necks deep within their prey's bodies, emerging slick with blood and viscera. They have razor-sharp beaks used to rip flesh from their victims and crack bones for the marrow within. The feet of these Undead scavengers are tipped with viciously hooked claws that can rend and tear their prey apart with frightening ease.

Carrion lived in the mountains to the east of Nehekhara and also the deserts to the west. Huge numbers of Carrion also nested in the towers and spires of Nehekhara's tomb-cities. After a great battle, with the slain strewn over the stricken field of war, the Carrion descended to feed in flocks so vast that they blotted out the light of the sun. According to inscriptions, the Carrion were sacred beasts, agents of Ualatp, the vulture-headed god of scavengers, who bore the spirits of lost warriors to the sky to fight in endless battles against the Daemons of darkness. This belief led to the Mortuary Cult burying corpses of Carrion in the necropolises, entombing many thousands of them within the pyramids of the Tomb Kings. At the will of the Liche Priests, these revered avian creatures are imbued with magical essence and once again take to the skies, their horrifying forms spreading fear amongst those who feel the chill of their shadow.

Once awakened from the slumber of death, the Carrion never again return to rest within the tombs and vaults of the pyramids. Instead, they soar above the lands of Nehekhara as they did in life, never tiring in their search for prey. Being primitive beasts, Carrion are driven by the need to feed their insatiable appetites, and they will go to great lengths to find their next meal. These ugly creatures learnt long ago that when armies clash they leave a swathe of corpses in their wake, and so when the Tomb Kings go to war, they are accompanied by great flocks of Carrion that circle high above.

Carrion will feast on the flesh of anything they can find. These scavengers are not fussy eaters and will gorge themselves on both freshly slaughtered corpses and cadavers that have festered for too long under the baking heat of the desert sun. Because of their immense size, Carrion will also prey upon the living. When Carrion hunger for live prey, they prefer to hunt the wounded and weakened, for in life they were notoriously cowardly birds, hesitant to battle foes that were able to fight back. When their victims are isolated and outnumbered, however, their ravenous hunger overcomes their craven nature and, with a hissing cry, they swoop down upon the enemy, eviscerating them with flurried swipes of their talons.

	M	WS	BS	S	T	W	I	A	LD
Carrion	2	3	0	4	4	2	3	3	4

TROOP TYPE: War Beast.

SPECIAL RULES: Fly, Nehekharan Undead.

"The Carrion of the Desert, whose mighty outstretched wings darken the sun on the day of slaughter."

- Climax of an invocation chant of the Liche Priests used at the Temple of the Sun in Khemri.

TOMB SWARMS

The tombs and pyramids of the necropolises are infested with the dried husks of scorpions, scarabs and countless other poisonous creatures of the desert. Though long dead, the mere presence of the Liche Priests and Tomb Kings fills their empty shells with animation, and they scuttle from their hiding places around the mortuary temples and beneath the scorched sands. The Liche Priests have long since gained mastery over these creatures, and they can summon them forth at will through their magical incantations. Thus, when the Tomb Kings' legions stride to war, they are accompanied by a scuttling swarm that spreads across the land in a black tide of crawling bodies. Those foolish enough to stand against a Tomb Swarm will drown beneath an unstoppable wave of Undead beetles, biting, clawing and burying themselves into the warmth of living flesh. Victims who gasp for air or cry out in fear are quickly silenced as a deluge of insects surge down their screaming throats, muffling cries of pain as they are devoured from the inside out.

Tomb Swarms are drawn to the magic animating the Undead, but it is to the Liche Priests and Tomb Kings that they are most keenly attracted. Not possessing a spirit of their own, they are easily controlled by the implacable will of the Tomb Kings. Left to their own devices, they revert to an instinctive lurking behaviour, making them ideal guards for the pyramids of slumbering Tomb Kings. Trespassers foolish enough to dislodge a capstone will find themselves quickly overwhelmed by a surging swarm of creatures. They are drawn to the warm blood of the living, trying to feed a hunger that no amount of flesh can ever sate. A Tomb Swarm's victims, poisoned by hundreds of bites and stings, are rapidly consumed as the vicious creatures eat through skin, clothing and bone alike.

There can be no escape from a Tomb Swarm, for the size of the creatures is such that they can crawl through the smallest of gaps without hindrance. Tomb Swarms can easily travel under the shifting sands of Nehekhara's desert and burrow beneath the feet of their unsuspecting prey. Without warning, a Tomb Swarm can errupt through cracks in the ground, flowing over the surface like a flood, dragging their victims kicking and screaming beneath the sands with the sheer weight of scuttling bodies.

Of all the dead creatures that make up the bulk of a Tomb Swarm, two had special significance in ancient Nehekharan society. The flesh-eating, skull-carapaced Khepra beetles were believed to be messengers of Usirian, god of the Underworld. They were his agents in the mortal world, and through their eyes would Usirian know the sins of all men. It was whispered that those who displeased Usirian were punished in death. Forbidden to enter the golden paradise of the afterlife, they were instead condemned to the lowest depths of the Netherworld where a hive of Khepra beetles would burrow into their immortal bodies and gnaw on their insides for all eternity. The other creature of importance was the black-clawed desert scorpion. The scorpion is the form chosen by Sokth, the god of treachery and murderers. Ancient Nehekharans believed that the scorpion would not sting one of Sokth's murderous followers, so those accused of killing another were pushed into a pit of scorpions. If a

victim somehow managed to survive his trial by scorpions and drag himself out of the pit, then it was taken as sign that they were indeed favoured by Sokth and hence guilty of their crime – the punishment for which was death by being thrown into a pit of snakes. Those who perished died in agony as scorpion venom coursed through their veins, but they were at least innocent.

	M	WS	BS	S	T	W	I	A	LD
Tomb Swarm	4	3	0	2	2	5	1	5	10

TROOP TYPE: Swarm.

SPECIAL RULES: Entombed Beneath the Sands, Nehekharan Undead, Poisoned Attacks.

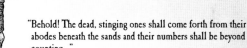

"Behold! The dead, stinging ones shall come forth from their abodes beneath the sands and their numbers shall be beyond counting..."

- Kharrahtut, Liche Priest of Quatar.

NECROPOLIS KNIGHTS

Necropolis Knights are elite warriors who ride atop giant snake-shaped statues. They are tethered to their mounts by a sharp hook, held firm in one mummified hand as the other wields a heavy spear that carves through mortal flesh. Their monstrous mounts shatter bones with every swipe of their tails and sink scimitar-sized fangs deep into soft flesh.

Necroserpents were built to guard the entranceways of the Mortuary Cult's temples. They are vast in stature, and even coiled they stand at least twice the height of a man. Though the Necroserpents standing sentinel outside some mortuary temples depict images of skull-vipers or double-headed blood-asps, the vast majority of these statues are created in the image of a hooded Khemrian cobra, for Qu'aph, the Nehekharan god of Cobras, took this as his corporeal form. Qu'aph was said to have preyed on the Dragons that dwelt in the Great Land before the coming of Man. The god would lie in ambush beneath the surface of the desert before lunging towards his prey and sinking his spear-sized fangs into their scaly throats. The venom of the Khemrian cobra is so potent that even a single drop is enough to kill a dozen warhorses or scores of fully grown men. Those bitten die with a rictus grin of agony on their faces as every muscle in their body contracts to the point where their own bones and teeth snap and break. The fangs of the Necroserpents mysteriously drip with this very same poison.

At the base of every Necroserpent is a pedestal in which there is a hollow alcove. Within each rests the sarcophagus of a Necropolis Knight. In their lifetimes, these warriors served in the sacred ranks of the Tomb Guard. They were all loyal soldiers and battle-scarred veterans, however, the constant years of violence and slaughter had become so deeply ingrained in these warriors' psyches that their bloodlust threatened to overcome their famed martial discipline. Such soldiers would break ranks without warning and could no longer be trusted to stand their ground whilst a foe still lived – actions that placed the life of the king in mortal jeopardy. When faced with the dishonour of exile, many committed ritual suicide, but some instead chose an agonising death for a chance to serve their king again in his eternal army. These brave soldiers would slit their palms and smear blood onto the belly of one of the giant Necroserpents before holding the wound under the venom dripping from their fangs. As the poison wracked their bodies, it was believed that Qu'aph would judge their souls, and those that were found worthy would be reborn in the next life as Necropolis Knights – warriors blessed with the skill, power and strength of the gods. Upon their death, these elite warriors were mummified and buried with their full panoply of war beneath the very same statue that they had sacrificed themselves before.

When Necropolis Knights are awakened to serve in the Tomb King's eternal army, the Necroserpents coiled above their resting places magically slither to unlife as well. Rider and mount are animated by the same warrior spirit, and they move as one being, riding to war in perfect ranks of terrifying cavalry. Necroserpents travel beneath the ground at a relentless pace, emerging from the depths with sand cascading off their forms, warriors standing proudly upon their hooded backs with spears lowered, ready to spill the blood of their foes. Serpentine bodies weave through the battlefield, blades, fangs and tails lashing out in all directions, leaving a trail of death and woe in their wake. There are few who can stand against the charge of a Necropolis Knight, for they are incredibly powerful and difficult to destroy. As mount and rider share the same soul, only by destroying both can an opponent truly defeat a Necropolis Knight. Few foes are equal to such a task.

	M	WS	BS	S	T	W	I	A	LD
Necropolis Knight	4	4	3	4	4	1	3	2	8
Necropolis Captain	4	4	3	4	4	1	3	3	8
Necroserpent	7	3	0	5	4	3	3	3	8

TROOP TYPE: Monstrous Cavalry.

SPECIAL RULES: Animated Construct, Killing Blow (Riders only), Nehekharan Undead, Poisoned Attacks (Necroserpents only).

Stone Hide: Necropolis Knights have a total armour save of 3+. This takes into account the combined effects of the mount's Animated Construct special rule, and the rider's armour and high vantage point.

SEPULCHRAL STALKERS

Sepulchral Stalkers were created by the ancient Nehekharans to delineate the borders of a king's realm. Over the centuries, the Sepulchral Stalkers have been swallowed by the shifting sands of the desert, and they now lie hidden beneath the dunes. Sepulchral Stalkers are statues that have the body of a snake and the upper torso of a man. Atop the statues' curved spines sit inhuman skulls, inside which glow eerie, baleful lights. Lying beneath the surface of the desert, they wait for intruders to pass by before launching a devastating ambush. When the trap is sprung, several horrifying, snake-like forms burst from the ground to surround their prey. The Sepulchral Stalkers impale their foes on ornate staves before they even realise they are under attack. However, it is not for the skill with which they wield these weapons that Sepulchral Stalkers are so feared, for those who gaze into their eyes are turned into pillars of sand, standing as still as statues themselves until a gust of wind blows them apart and scatters the grains into the desert.

The incantations required to awaken Sepulchral Stalkers are complicated and difficult. First, a Liche Priest must collect the remains of a fallen Nehekharan warrior, one whose skeletal body is broken beyond all hopes of repair. The Liche Priests then walk out into the open desert under a full-moon, where they scatter these fragments on the ground, casting powdered bone to the wind as they speak a magical

incantation. At the ritual's end, they throw the eyes of a desert cockatrice onto the sand, and the offerings sink beneath the desert surface. The spirits of the warriors' remains are thus bound into the stone frame of one of the buried Sepulchral Stalkers. They are imbued with powerful enchantments and compelled to patrol the lands against invaders for all eternity.

Sepulchral Stalkers can burrow underneath the desert as quickly as they can move across its surface. They are instinctive hunters who can sense their prey trudging across the ground above, and they can prepare their ambushes without ever being seen. Those who are foolish enough to face Sepulchral Stalkers are magically transformed into sand. Even foes who only catch a momentary glimpse of these creatures may find that one of their limbs crumbles in a shower of golden grains before their eyes – those that stare any longer seal their own doom. Sepulchral Stalkers are said to be the desert's vengeance made manifest, and as suddenly as an attack begins, it ends. A lucky survivor might just witness the tip of a tail burrowing back under the dunes as the Sepulchral Stalkers leave in search of other prey.

It is claimed by foolhardy heroes that a Sepulchral Stalker can be tricked into staring at its own reflection, for these monsters are not immune to the sorcerous enchantments of their own stares; rumours abound that they can be defeated with only a polished breastplate or a mirrored shield. However, it is perhaps safer to attempt to creep up behind a Sepulchral Stalker and strike off its head, but even then care must be taken not to look at the decapitated beast, for in death, a vestigial hint of arcane power remains in their infernal eyes.

	M	WS	BS	S	T	W	I	A	LD
Sepulchral Stalker	7	3	3	4	4	3	3	2	8

TROOP TYPE: Monstrous Beast.

SPECIAL RULES: Animated Construct, Entombed Beneath the Sands, Nehekharan Undead.

Transmogrifying Gaze: This is a shooting attack with the following profile:

Range	Strength	Special
8"	1	See below.

A Transmogrifying Gaze is a magical attack, and does not require a roll To Hit. Instead, when the unit shoots, roll an artillery dice for each Sepulchral Stalker in the unit and add the results together. The target suffers a number of automatic hits equal to the result. When rolling To Wound with these hits, substitute the target's Toughness with its Initiative value. If the target has several Initiative values, always use the highest. Targets with no Initiative value are immune to this attack. No armour saves are allowed against a Transmogrifying Gaze. Finally, for each Misfire result rolled, the Sepulchral Stalkers suffer D3 automatic Wounds with no armour saves allowed, as they catch glimpses of their own reflection in their foe's sword blades or polished shields.

USHABTI

Carved into the likenesses of the gods and goddesses of Nehekhara, Ushabti stand as guardian statues around the perimeters of the necropolises and within the passageways of the great pyramids of the Tomb Kings. Ushabti are imposing monuments, and all who pass through their shadows tremble. In times of need, the Liche Priests awaken the Ushabti with powerful incantations, and with the sound of cracking stone, the Ushabti step down from their plinths and daises, silent and ready for war. In ancient times, the living warriors of Nehekhara took great strength from the fact that the Ushabti fought alongside them, for who could fail to be inspired by the physical representations of their gods marching into battle at their sides?

It was the ancient Nehekharans' belief that their gods and goddesses dwelt in the Great Land before the birth of Man. It is said that the span of the deities' lives numbered in the thousands of years. After this golden era, when gods walked as men, they became invisible spirits, able to take on any form they desired. Thus it was that Asaph, the beautiful goddess of vengeance and magic, chose the form of the asp, while others chose the crocodile, the lion, the vulture or some other fearsome animal of the desert. Most depictions of the gods in this grand pantheon show them in these powerful forms, and their visages are commonly carved as guardian Ushabti in the necropolises of Nehekhara. Some of

the most common statues depict the image of Djaf, the jackal-headed god of war and the dead, and Phakth, the hawk-faced deity of the sky whose piercing gaze is said to be able to see the sins of the deceased. Sculpted from stone, marble and even jade, this magnificent statuary is decorated with filigreed gold and dazzling polished jewels.

The rituals needed to animate these towering god-statues are far more difficult and complex than those needed to awaken the legions of Skeleton Warriors. As a result, Ushabti are far more resilient than the skeletal warriors of the Tomb King's eternal army, and their warrior-spirits are bound with far more powerful magic.

In the ancient language of Nehekhara, the name Ushabti translates literally as 'chosen of the gods'. Indeed, the divinities do not consent to any mere mortal inhabiting statues made in their image. Only the most powerful souls, those of particularly brave warriors and heroic champions, are judged worthy enough to animate an Ushabti's sculpted form. Thus, Ushabti are possessed by the souls of Nehekhara's mightiest heroes. Ushabti stride through the battlefield like gods of war, infused with the temperament and strength of their form's pantheon deity. Their statuesque bodies can withstand enormous damage, and they are incredibly strong. With a single hand, an Ushabti is capable of crushing an enemy's steel helmet, and its contents, with contemptuous ease.

Ushabti wield huge ritualistic weapons, from large-bladed staves that would take the combined strength of three mortal men to lift, to great bows that fire arrows the size of spears. These mighty weapons are as elaborately crafted and decorated as the Ushabti who brandish them, their gilded surfaces engraved by a dozen sculptors with intricate patterns and hieroglyphs. In battle, Ushabti wield their massive weapons effortlessly. Every sweeping arc of their blades cutting a bloody swathe through their foes and every arrow fired punching through their targets in an explosion of bone and gore.

	M	WS	BS	S	T	W	I	A	LD
Ushabti	5	4	2	4	4	3	3	3	8
Ushabti Ancient	5	4	2	4	4	3	3	4	8

TROOP TYPE: Monstrous Infantry.

SPECIAL RULES: Animated Construct, Arrows of Asaph, Nehekharan Undead.

EQUIPMENT
Great Bows: The spear-sized arrows fired from these mighty bows can punch through an armoured knight with ease, and inflict grievous wounds on even the toughest foes.

Great bows are missile weapons with the following profile:

Range	Strength	Special
30"	6	Volley Fire.

TOMB SCORPIONS

Tomb Scorpions are powerful creations of the Mortuary Cult, formed from a combination of stone, metal, lacquered wood and fused bone. Burrowing beneath the surface of the desert, they attack suddenly and without warning, exploding into the fray in a shower of sand. They are lethal foes, for a Tomb Scorpion's tail carries a potent sting that can incapacitate the largest foes, and they have powerful pincers that can slice a man in half. As they scuttle forward on eight segmented legs, they hack apart anything in their path.

Tomb Scorpions are carved and moulded into the representations of the giant, mythical scorpions that are said to guard the entrance to the Nehekharan Underworld. These fabled creatures are said to protect the Realm of Souls from the predations of dark Daemons who wish to feed upon the spirits of dead kings.

Tomb Scorpions also serve as sarcophagi, for the shell of each construct is formed around the cadaverous body of an ancient Liche Priest. Although Liche Priests are unable to die a natural death, many have perished through wounds sustained in battle. Those that fall are embalmed and interred within a Tomb Scorpion. Canopic jars containing their vital organs, or what withered remains are left of them, are embedded within the scorpion-tombs in a ritualistic pattern that symbolises death. However, some remnant of a Liche Priest's spirit always remains trapped within their mummified corpses. Through incantations, these embers are rekindled, infusing the inanimate shells of the Tomb Scorpions with power. This magical source also provides Tomb Scorpions with a degree of protection against the spells of enemy wizards, whose sorcerous bolts of energy unravel and fade as they are absorbed harmlessly by the Undead constructs' carapaces.

Each scorpion-shaped sarcophagus is inscribed with hieroglyphs of preservation, and a ceremony of awakening is spoken by a Liche Priest to animate to them. If the ritual has been performed correctly, the Tomb Scorpion will become infused with the residual power of the corpse within it. This ritual is exceptionally complex and lasts from moonrise until the first rays of dawn. The slightest mistake or mispronunciation can have dire consequences; a swarm of Undead scorpions may burst out of the desert and sting the Liche Priest to death, or desert spirits may turn the wizard's body inside out and feast on his withered remains. At the very least the ritual will fail and must be recited from the very beginning. Occasionally, despite every syllable being uttered correctly, some of these ancient ones no longer respond to the incantations of awakening. That these constructs are truly dead is doubtful, as a spark of power can still be felt radiating from their carapaces. Rather, it is thought that by binding their souls to the mortal plane, the Liche Priests cheated the god of the Underworld out of his rightful due. Thus it is thought that this jealous deity is not always willing to give up his long awaited prizes by allowing the spirits of Liche Priests to leave the Realm of Souls.

When the Tomb Kings go to war, the Liche Priests send out their magical call and summon the Tomb Scorpions into wakefulness. Those Tomb Scorpions that respond to the incantations will travel for leagues beneath the ground before clawing their way to the surface and falling upon their enemies with razor-sharp claws and stinging tails. It is a truly terrifying sight to behold the sands parting to reveal the monstrous form of a Tomb Scorpion, and very often, the last thing their enemies will ever witness.

	M	WS	BS	S	T	W	I	A	LD
Tomb Scorpion	7	4	0	5	5	3	3	4	8

TROOP TYPE: Monstrous Beast.

SPECIAL RULES: Animated Construct, Entombed Beneath the Sands, Killing Blow, Magic Resistance (1), Nehekharan Undead, Poisoned Attacks.

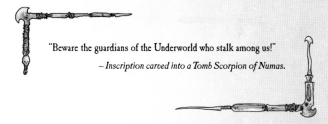

"Beware the guardians of the Underworld who stalk among us!"

– *Inscription carved into a Tomb Scorpion of Numas.*

KHEMRIAN WARSPHINX

Khemrian Warsphinxes are giant leonine statues that wade through the ranks of their foes, crushing them underfoot as if they were nothing more than bothersome insects. They are almost impervious to harm, and their stone-hard hides protect them from all but the truest strikes; anything less than a direct hit from a war machine is likely to glance harmlessly away. Atop each Khemrian Warsphinx is an ornate howdah in which several Tomb Guard ride. These elite warriors direct their mount's actions as if it were an extension of their own mummified bodies, laying into the foes below with great, double-handed spears.

Warsphinxes were first constructed in Khemri to guard the entranceways to the kings' inner sanctums. Over time, the rulers of other cities demanded similar guardians, and before long Warsphinxes stood sentry within every burial pyramid. Here, inside the vast amphitheatre chambers, they are said to roam, preying on intruders whilst the king slumbers. Some kings even had a Warsphinx constructed to stand watch over their own sacred sarcophagi, and these were especially lavish and ornate. Upon awakening, a Tomb King would ride his royal Warsphinx into battle, leading his army out of the burial chambers and into the blinding light of day.

As with any Nehekharan sculpture, no two Khemrian Warsphinxes are quite alike. The Necrotects were always looking to build grander and more impressive creations than those of their predecessors. Some Warsphinxes have scorpion tails filled with potent venom, whilst others breathe fire, immolating their foes in blazing conflagrations. It is rare indeed for a new Khemrian Warsphinx to be constructed, and most of those that are seen prowling alongside the Tomb Kings' armies have existed for thousands of years. If one of these giant constructs is somehow destroyed in battle, its sacred pieces are gathered up by skeletal work gangs and dragged back to the cities of Nehekhara to be restored and resculpted by the Necrotects of the necropolises.

Khemrian Warsphinxes are terrifying foes to face, and enemies that do not flee before them are swatted aside by stone claws or torn apart by fanged jaws. However, this is just a fraction of their full destructive power. When a Khemrian Warsphinx rears up above its prey, those lurking in its shadow are doomed. As the leonine monster crashes down, it smashes its boulder-sized limbs into the ground with appalling force. The resultant shockwave knocks foes off their feet, pulping organs and splintering bones. Those that survive this earth-shattering impact find themselves in a crater of broken, twisted bodies. However, there can be no hope for anything caught directly underneath the point of impact. All that remains of these crushed unfortunates is a fine, red mist that sprays over the victim's stunned comrades.

	M	WS	BS	S	T	W	I	A	LD
Khemrian Warsphinx	6	4	0	5	8	5	1	4	8
Tomb Guard Crew	-	3	3	4	-	-	3	1	8

TROOP TYPE: Monster.

SPECIAL RULES: Animated Construct, Killing Blow (Tomb Guard Crew only), Large Target, Nehekharan Undead, Terror.

Thundercrush Attack: After its crew have attacked, a Khemrian Warsphinx may exchange all of its Attacks to make a single Thundercrush Attack (though it can still Thunderstomp). Roll To Hit against the highest Weapon Skill amongst the enemy models in base contact. If this Attack hits, place the small template anywhere so that it is touching the Khemrian Warsphinx's base. Any infantry, war beasts or swarm models that lie underneath the template (friend or foe!) suffer a single Strength 3 hit. The model under the template's central hole instead suffers a single Strength 9 hit with the Multiple Wounds (D3) special rule. Other troop types underneath the template are too big to be crushed, and don't suffer any hits.

Howdah Crew: Unless the Khemrian Warsphinx is taken as a mount for a character, it is ridden by four Tomb Guard Crew. Like a chariot, the monster and its howdah crew have their own characteristics, but are treated as a single model.

When moving, the model always uses the Movement characteristic of the Khemrian Warsphinx. The Khemrian Warsphinx and Tomb Guard crew use their own Weapon Skill, Strength, Initiative and Attacks characteristics when they attack. Each can attack any opponent that the model is in base contact with.

All hits upon the Khemrian Warsphinx are resolved using the monster's Toughness and Wounds, and use its save. In combat, enemy models attacking the Khemrian Warsphinx roll against the monster's Weapon Skill when rolling To Hit.

Apart from these exceptions, a Khemrian Warsphinx is treated as a monster in all respects, as described in the Warhammer rulebook. A Khemrian Warsphinx can be taken as a ridden monster for a Tomb King or a Tomb Prince who will replace all the Tomb Guard Crew. In this case, shooting attacks against it will hit the monster on the D6 roll of 1-4, and the character on a roll of 5+, as normal.

UPGRADES:
Envenomed Sting: Many statues have a scorpion's sting, dripping with a virulent poison that can boil a victim's blood.

All Attacks made by a model with this upgrade have the Poisoned Attacks special rule. This does not affect the Attacks made by the crew, mounted characters (if any are present), Thundercrush Attacks or Thunderstomps.

Fiery Roar: A Khemrian Warsphinx's ferocious roar is born from the heat of a thousand funeral pyres.

A Khemrian Warsphinx with this upgrade has a Strength 4 Breath Weapon with the Flaming Attacks special rule.

THE CRIMSON KING

Imrathepis, the Crimson King of Numas, was an aggressive and brilliant general. His stalwart legions were easily recognised by their blood-red banners and shields, and Imrathepis himself rode to war atop a magnificent Khemrian Warsphinx whose flanks were deep scarlet. In his mortal lifetime, King Imrathepis fought beside Alcadizaar the Conqueror, and he was one of the great ruler's chief lieutenants. The Crimson King was present during many pivotal battles, including the of subjugation of Ka-Sabar, the pacification of the Black Boar Orc tribes and the sacking of cursed Lahmia, where Imrathepis bested several Vampires in personal combat.

In undeath, King Imrathepis' thirst for battle was no longer tempered by the wisdom of Alcadizaar. Upon awakening from his sacred sarcophagus, the Crimson King immediately set about reclaiming the lands he had conquered in centuries past. Imrathepis and his legions swept north through the Badlands like a hurricane of blood. From atop the armoured platform of his Khemrian Warsphinx, the Crimson King slew scores of greenskin savages. Imrathepis would lead every charge from the front, driving his curved, golden-edged blade deep into the flesh of his enemies as his Khemrian Warsphinx, dripping with the blood of the slaughtered, waded through the hordes of Orcs and pulped their bodies underfoot. The impetuous king then drove his Undead legions eastwards into the Mountains of Mourn, forging through the wind-swept passes in search of more foes to vanquish.

King Imrathepis' arrogance was to be his undoing, and he was finally defeated by the Ogres of the Thunderhoof Tribe. Imrathepis mistakenly believed the Ogres to be nothing more than simple brutes. The Crimson King was therefore completely unprepared when the Ogres ambushed the Undead by unleashing a herd of stampeding Rhinoxes within the narrow confines of Daggertooth Valley. The skeletal warriors of the Crimson King's legions were crushed to powdered bone by the great cave beasts, and only Imrathepis, standing atop his carmine Warsphinx, survived. Though his mount had been buffeted and its stone body was cracked, the great Khemrian Warsphinx did not yield. Alas, Imrathepis was now alone and surrounded by the entire Ogre tribe. Howling a curse, the Crimson King and his battered mount drove on regardless, smiting a score of Ogres before finally succumbing to the hammer-blows of the tribe's Ironguts. After the battle, the Ogre's Tyrant, Folgut the Corpulent, snapped the Tomb King's leg off and fashioned it into a toothpick before returning to his mountain lair.

However, the royal line of King Imrathepis did not end there, and Prince Rakaph III, dynastic heir to the Crimson King, set off from Numas a mere decade later to enact his father's revenge. Rakaph III led not one, but a dozen Khemrian Warsphinxes into the Mountains of Mourn to destroy the Thunderhoof Ogres. The hulking leonine statues trekked to the summit of Cragg Rock, which overlooked the Ogres lair, before battering their stone limbs into the mountainside, causing a titanic avalanche that buried the entire Thunderhoof Tribe beneath several thousand tons of rock and ice.

NECROSPHINX

Necrosphinxes are nightmarish beasts of destruction that glide through the air in bounding leaps before falling amongst their terrified prey, scything down the living as mortals reap the wheat of the field. None can stand against such terrifying beings, and only when all before them have been butchered will they stop.

A Necrosphinx is a bizarre and horrifying statue – a strange amalgamation of the mythical beasts that are said to inhabit the Nehekharan Underworld, maintaining order amongst the honoured dead. A Necrosphinx has a torso and face of a man, and is armed with gigantic, scything blades that can sever the neck of a Dragon in a single slice. Many also have a scorpion-like tail, better enabling them to stand sentry against the predations of evil. Finally, sprouting from the statue's back are a pair of ornate wings which mimic those of the falcons that circle the highest levels of the Underworld, keeping watch so that the souls of the damned may not escape. It was believed that by combining all these forms the ancient Nehekharans were creating the ultimate warrior, one that possessed the strength to destroy all their enemies. However, many of the Mortuary Cult's Liche Priests believed these sculptures to be an abomination, whose presence would curse the land, for surely such beasts had no right to exist on the mortal plane. Following a century of plague and famine, the superstitious kings of Nehekhara agreed that the Necrosphinxes were to

blame, but none dared destroy them in case it angered the gods of the Underworld. Instead, vast pits were dug in the desert in which the Necrosphinxes were buried and all but forgotten with the passage of time.

A Necrosphinx did not see the light of day again until millennia later, when a mighty Orc Waaagh! swept down from the Badlands into Nehekhara. The greenskin horde attacked with a score of monstrous Wyverns at their head, destroying everything in their path. As the Waaagh! pushed towards Khemri, Settra himself ordered the Mortuary Cult to reawaken the ancient Necrosphinxes. More fearful of Settra's wrath than anything else, the cowering Liche Priests obeyed and began a week-long magical ceremony. Upon the ritual's completion, a deep rumble reverberated throughout the desert. Moments later, fountains of bone-dry earth exploded from the ground as a dozen Necrosphinxes broke the surface. Without pause, the stone monsters pounced upon the greenskins, slaughtering the savages with every sweep of their massive claws. Not even the mighty Wyverns could halt their murderous rampage, for the nightmarish statues cut through the greenskin's monsters' thick, scaly necks with single strokes of their razor sharp pincers. All Necrosphinxes have since been reclaimed from the desert sands to stand proudly in the sun once more, forming an important part of the Tomb King's eternal army, and wherever they travel they spread death and destruction.

The Liche Priests do not think that a Necrosphinx is animated by the soul of a valiant warrior like the other war-statues that walk beside the Tomb King's skeletal legions. Instead, they believe that the sinister gods, Pha'a and Usekph, breathed life into these horrifying creations. These malevolent deities are said to dwell within mighty tombs beneath the sands, buried by the other gods for their destructive ways. If the Liche Priests are right, then the mysterious gods have finally found a means by which to vent their fury upon the world. Whatever the truth, deep within every Necrosphinx is the burning need to destroy, and the incantations of servitude laid upon them are the only things that keep them from turning upon their creators and tearing Nehekhara asunder.

	M	WS	BS	S	T	W	I	A	LD
Necrosphinx	6	4	0	5	8	5	1	5	8

TROOP TYPE: Monster.

SPECIAL RULES: Animated Construct, Fly, Killing Blow, Large Target, Nehekharan Undead, Terror.

Decapitating Strike: Before rolling To Hit, nominate one of the Necrosphinx's Attacks to be made with the Decapitating Strike ability, and roll it separately. This special Attack strikes at Strength 10 and has the Heroic Killing Blow special rule.

UPGRADES:
A Necrosphinx may take the Envenomed Sting upgrade, which works exactly as described on page 49.

NECROLITH COLOSSUS

Towering over the Tomb King's skeletal legions, mighty statues of venerated heroes and ancient kings stride to battle. These stone giants are the Necrolith Colossi, and none can stand against them.

In ancient times, before the rise of Settra and the founding of the Mortuary Cult, many were the legends of beings of immense stature that walked the land. According to half-forgotten inscriptions, these giant warriors were left by Nehekhara's gods to stand watch over the lands, immortal sentinels who would guard their realms against evil Daemons. So it is thought that the most ancient of the Necrolith Colossi were created by the gods themselves. However, the ancient Nehekharans constructed countless more – hewing their forms from mighty pillars of rock and carving them directly into the faces of cliffs and pyramids. Every necropolis in Nehekhara is now watched over by at least one of these imposing figures. Outside the ancient cities, Necrolith Colossi stand as motionless sentries, guarding important valley entrances and gateways from rampaging monsters and enemy warbands for aeons at a time.

Made to resemble immense heroes of old, Necrolith Colossi stand noble and proud. Their forms are covered in skulls, bones and mortuary ornamentation. Indeed, such was Nehekhara's obsession with death and immortality that some

Colossi have even been carved to resemble giant skeletons. Breastplates, vambraces and sometimes great crested helmets were hammered onto the stone bodies of these constructs, each lavishly decorated and engraved.

As the skill of the priesthood grew, they turned their talents towards binding the souls of Nehekhara's foremost warriors into these vast statues, for who could face such a creation in battle? The incantations of summoning required were long and arduous, demanding the combined power of a score of Liche Priests. Such is the magic instilled into Necrolith Colossi that once spirits are bound within their mighty frames, they will never again need the incantations of Liche Priests to prompt them into wakefulness. Necrolith Colossi will react immediately to the presence of unwelcome strangers and move to strike them down. Stirring from their vigil, they shake loose the sand and dust that has settled on their immense forms and stride relentlessly towards the intruders.

A Necrolith Colossus is armed with traditional weapons and armour, only on a massive scale, carrying vast bows or giant swords that stand taller than a Troll. A Necrolith Colossus is a supremely powerful foe, and its weapons can carve through an armoured knight and his barded steed in a single stroke. In battle, Necrolith Colossi are terrifying to behold. The desert itself trembles at their passing, the impacts of their heavy footfalls sounding a mighty drumbeat that heralds impending doom. They are nigh impossible to stop, crushing foes beneath their feet and sending dead and broken bodies flying in all directions.

THE WAR-STATUARY OF NEHEKHARA

It was not just the elite soldiery of Nehekhara's legions that achieved great status in ancient times. The names of countless war-statues are recorded on the surfaces of tombs and sarcophagi as well.

The Bone Giants of Bhagar were such creations, magnificent Necrolith Colossi whose bodies and limbs were carved from a white marble said to be indistinguishable from actual bone. Time and again the Bone Giants strode out to battle, and not even the bravest heroes could stand against these skull-faced giants of death. The Alabaster Army of Quatar was perhaps even more feared, for their ivory ranks crushed whole armies underfoot. These towering Ushabti fought like the gods they portrayed, and they would return after a battle won to stand once more in the alcoves of the White Palace, their flanks still slick with the blood of the slain.

The Emerald Sentinels of Lybaras, the Golden Warsphinx of King Anubekh, the Skull Guardian of the Charnel Valley, the list of legendary constructs goes on. However, all these statues are said to be eclipsed by the size and majesty of the Hieroscorpion of Khemri, whose titanic form, as large as a burial pyramid, was forged from jet obsidian and blood-cooled bronze. This gargantuan creation prowls the deserts to this day, preying on any who dare trespass into the Land of the Dead.

	M	WS	BS	S	T	W	I	A	LD
Necrolith Colossus	6	3	2	6	6	5	1	4	8

TROOP TYPE: Monster.

SPECIAL RULES: Animated Construct, Arrows of Asaph, Large Target, Nehekharan Undead, Terror.

Unstoppable Assault: In the turn in which a Necrolith Colossus charges, every unsaved Wound that it inflicts in close combat immediately allows it to make an additional Attack. Note that these additional Attacks also benefit from the Unstoppable Assault rule, but Thunderstomps do not.

EQUIPMENT
Bow of the Desert: Only the Necrolith Colossi can wield these massive bows, which fire enormous arrows that rip through the ranks of the enemy.

A bow of the desert is a Bolt Thrower with the profile shown below. The Attack can be made even if the Necrolith Colossus moves.

Range	Strength	Special
48"	6	Multiple Wounds (D3).

Armour saves are not permitted against Wounds caused by a bow of the desert.

HIEROTITANS

A Hierotitan is a gigantic animated statue whose face is carved in the likeness of one of the Nehekharan deities of death. These idols radiate a sinister aura of magic, and it is said that those who stand within their shadow can hear the cruel laughter of ancient gods.

Hierotitans were constructed to stand within the uppermost chambers of the Tomb Kings' burial pyramids. It was believed that they would act as spirit guides for the souls of deceased kings, responsible for ushering the eternal sprits of monarchs between the mortal world and the Realm of Souls.

No expense was spared in sculpting a Hierotitan, a towering effigy whose form was lavished with gold and gems. In one hand, a Hierotitan carries an elaborate staff, which bears the hieroglyph of the sun god and lights the Hierotitan's path as it walks in the abyss that separates the mortal world from the Realm of Souls. This light wards away the evil spirits that dwell in the dark, Daemons who would otherwise prey on the souls of those wandering the void. The Hierotitan's other hand grasps a giant pair of scales. According to legends, it is upon these scales that the king's soul is judged by the god of the Underworld to see if it is worthy enough to enter the realm of the honoured dead, or whether it is to be cast into the fiery pits of the Netherworld. Both these items are wrought with powerful incantations, for the fate of the king's eternal spirit depends upon them. In battle, the Hierotitan can infuse his staff with the light of the sun god, causing those caught in the dazzling rays to burst into flames. Likewise, the Hierotitan can unleash the power contained within its foreboding scales, and ethereal claws will stretch out and rip their foes' souls from their bodies.

Interred within the chest of a Hierotitan is the mummified body of an ancient priest. These were the high priests of the Mortuary Cult that lived and died as mortal men, before the time when their knowledge was such that they could walk the lands of Nehekhara for all time. In their lifetime, these priests studied the art of communion with the gods. Thus, as they served their king in life, so their soul would continue to serve him in death. It is the magically attuned spirit of the deceased priest that allows the Hierotitan to walk in two worlds at once, acting as a conduit between the two realms.

To a Hierotitan, the world appears as a dream. Their very presence on the battlefield creates a direct link between the mortal world and the Realm of Souls through which the gods hear the rituals of the Liche Priests. When a Hierotitan strides across the land, the incantations of the Mortuary Cult are leant great power. Entire regiments of enemy soldiers are dragged beneath the sands at the uttering of the simplest incantation, and a single syllable read from a magical scroll can summon a vast plague of desert locusts that envelops and consumes their foes.

	M	WS	BS	S	T	W	I	A	LD
Hierotitan	6	3	0	6	6	5	1	3	8

TROOP TYPE: Monster.

SPECIAL RULES: Animated Construct, Large Target, Nehekharan Undead, Terror.

Spirit Conduit: Hierotitans act as magical loci for the army's Liche Priests. While a friendly Nehekharan Undead Wizard is within 12" of one or more Hierotitans adds +D3 to the casting result of each spell he attempts to cast (roll for the bonus each time).

EQUIPMENT:
Icon of Ptra: *An Icon of Ptra is said to illuminate the path to the Realm of Souls with the sun god's own light.*

Bound Spell (power level 3). An Icon of Ptra contains the spell *Shem's Burning Gaze* (see the Lore of Light).

Scales of Usirian: *The souls of those who gaze upon the Scales of Usirian are judged by the god of the Underworld, and those that are found unworthy are condemned to oblivion.*

Bound Spell (power level 4). The Scales of Usirian contain the spell *Spirit Leech* (see the Lore of Death).

THE CRATER OF THE WAKING DEAD

Such was the rivalry between King Imanotep of Mahrak and King Ushtep of Rasetra that they drove their Undead legions across the desert to end a feud that mortal death had not settled.

The two armies clashed in a giant crater situated between the two cities, and the mummified rulers met in personal combat beside a half-buried Hierotitan. The Tomb Kings dueled for hours, but their immortal bodies never grew weary and the thrill of battle soon ebbed to be replaced with a joyless bitterness. In frustration, the warring Tomb Kings vented their anger upon the gods, blaming them for their cursed existence and uttering a string of insults. These words did not go by unheard, for the Hierotitan in whose shadow the monarchs were fighting was literally a conduit between the mortal plane and the Realm of Souls. The deities heard the profanities as clearly as if they had been uttered to their faces, and their anger was great.

The gods cursed the rival Tomb Kings to wage an endless war. Countless thousands of skeletal warriors now battle across the vast crater, chariots smashing into each other and crushing their foes into the dust. However, the crater is saturated with magical energy, and the instant a Skeleton is cut down its broken bones mend anew and the warrior staggers to its feet, ready to continue the fight. The battle has now raged for over three millennia, and in the centre of the crater are the two ancient kings – locked in a perpetual duel. It is said that a hundred Hierotitans now line the crater's edge and the gods themselves watch the eternal war unfold through their eyes.

SETTRA THE IMPERISHABLE
THE GREAT KING OF NEHEKHARA

Settra the Imperishable is the King of all Tomb Kings. He is a ruthless leader whose thirst for conquest knows no bounds. Settra's power is far greater than any other Tomb King, and his unyielding will is such that he never needs to return to his sarcophagus to rest. Instead, he chooses to remain awake, the ruler of a devastated land. The immortality he lusted after in life is now his, and the civilisations that flourished in his absence feel his wrath.

Settra rides to war upon his magical chariot, the Crown of Nehekhara resting majestically upon his head as a symbol of his might. Settra is a bloodthirsty and skilled warrior, and he drives his enemies before him without pity, scything through the ranks of mortals with every sweep of his blessed blade.

Settra alone among the Tomb Kings knows the secrets of the Liche Priests. He understands their language, but to his eternal frustration, Settra has never been able to fully master their magical arts. Though he has not forgiven the Mortuary Cult for their lies, Settra still has need of their abilities to summon forth his vassal kings and maintain his realm. However, it is a foolish Liche Priest who thinks he can wield power over the King of Khemri. Any that invite Settra's wrath, Liche Priest or otherwise, are torn limb from limb.

	M	WS	BS	S	T	W	I	A	LD
Settra the Imperishable	4	7	3	6	5	4	3	5	10
Chariot of the Gods	-	-	-	5	5	5	-	-	-
Skeletal Steed	8	2	-	3	-	-	2	1	-

TROOP TYPE:
Infantry (Special Character; Tomb King & Liche Priest).

MAGIC: Settra the Imperishable is a Level 1 Wizard. He uses spells from the Lore of Nehekhara.

SPECIAL RULES: The Curse (see page 30), Flammable, My Will Be Done (see page 30), Nehekharan Undead.

Settra the Great: If you take Settra the Imperishable, he must be your army's General. Settra's Inspiring Presence has a range of 18".

MAGIC ITEMS:
The Crown of Nehekhara: *Incorporating several crowns into one, this regal headdress allows Settra to instil his unyielding will into all those nearby.*

Enchanted Item. Settra the Imperishable's My Will Be Done special rule affects all friendly Nehekharan Undead units within 6" of him, not just the unit he has joined.

The Chariot of the Gods: *This mighty chariot carries with it the blessings of all the gods and goddesses of Nehekhara, and its wheels blaze with mystical flame.*

Enchanted Item. Settra rides a scythed chariot drawn by four skeletal steeds. Its profile can be found above. Impact Hits from the Chariot of the Gods are magical attacks that have the Flaming Attacks special rule. The Chariot of the Gods has an armour save of 4+.

The Scarab Brooch of Usirian: *Made in the image of a skull-carapaced khepra beetle, this talisman surrounds the wearer with the protective energies of Usirian, god of the Underworld.*

Talisman. The Scarab Brooch of Usirian grants Settra the Imperishable and the Chariot of the Gods a 4+ ward save and the Magic Resistance (1) special rule.

The Blessed Blade of Ptra: *This revered weapon has been blessed by the sun god, Ptra. The blade's white-hot edge, infused with the heat of the desert sun, sets the air itself ablaze, and glows so brightly that it blinds Settra's foes.*

Magic Weapon. Hits from the Blessed Blade of Ptra have the Flaming Attacks special rule. Armour saves cannot be taken against Wounds caused by this weapon. In addition, a character or monster that suffers one or more unsaved Wounds from the Blessed Blade of Ptra suffers -1 to its rolls To Hit (both shooting and close combat) for the remainder of the game.

THE HERALD NEKAPH
EMISSARY OF SETTRA

Nekaph is Settra's chosen herald, his personal champion and most trusted servant, loyal unto death and beyond into the next life. When Settra left the mortal realm, Nekaph was the first to commit suicide, and his body was entombed beside his lord. When Settra the Imperishable awoke from his centuries of slumber, Nekaph's mummified form was already standing by, prepared to fulfil his king's indomitable will and smite his enemies once more.

The Herald Nekaph was not born of noble birth. Indeed it was whispered that he was not even born of Nehekharan blood and that his parents were from the uncivilised tribes to the north of the Great Land. Thus, as Nekaph grew into a man and joined the legions of Khemri's army, he was considered by all to be little more than an uncouth barbarian. Despite his heritage, however, Nekaph's strength, feats of skill and unswerving loyalty to his king were unsurpassed. Nekaph distinguished himself in battle time and again, and before his eighteenth year he was inducted into the prestigious ranks of the elite Tomb Guard. Within two years, Nekaph had risen to command Settra's royal guard, and soon after he was appointed as his personal herald, for there was no more incorruptible a warrior in all of Nehekhara. As a mark of Settra's trust in his chosen champion, Nekaph was gifted the Flail of Skulls – an unmistakable symbol of Settra's power and a weapon that the ruler of Khemri himself once wielded on the field of battle.

Nekaph was a formidable man in life, renowned for his powerful physique and uncompromising sense of duty. Even unarmed, Nekaph was deadly, and he could cave in the skulls of his opponent's with a single blow of his fist. Though he slew many enemies at the behest of Settra, it was only when he fought duels on behalf of his king that the Herald Nekaph's true warrior potential was reached, for he would fight all the harder knowing that the honour of his lord was at stake – something far more important than his own life. Nekaph would deflect the blows of his opponent with consummate skill before delivering a fatal blow of his own. Nekaph was not only a mighty warrior, he was also possessed of a great intelligence. This is an essential quality in any Tomb Herald, for they must be able to remember their lord's many and elaborate titles. Indeed, such was Settra's power and achievements that reciting his entire list of titles took Nekaph almost two hours.

Nekaph rides from city to city, as he did in life, at the head of one of Settra's eternal legions. When they arrive at the enemy's gates, Nekaph halts and demands an audience with the city's rulers. When the cowering leaders come forth, the Emissary of Settra addresses them and offers them a single chance to surrender. Though his jaw does not move, and no discernable sound ushers from his lipless mouth, Nekaph's trembling foes hear a deep voice echoing in their heads. Rulers of nations quake with fear as Nekaph demands their fealty, and they realise that their doom has arrived. Those that refuse to kneel before the might of Settra, or those that foolishly choose to attack Nekaph's assembled legion, must face the unbridled wrath of Khemri. Leading from the front, Nekaph advances towards his foes, smashing them asunder with every blow of the Flail of Skulls. As the bodies of the enemy stack up and the Undead legions continue their implacable advance, the defenders realise the futility of their resistance – but the Herald Nekaph shows no mercy. The time for surrender has long since passed, for once battle has been joined no parley can be entered into. Defiance is met only with death and, at the battle's end, the skull of another conquered king will hang from Nekaph's magical flail.

	M	WS	BS	S	T	W	I	A	LD
The Herald Nekaph	4	5	3	4	4	2	3	3	8

TROOP TYPE: Infantry (Special Character; Tomb Herald).

SPECIAL RULES: Flammable, Killing Blow, Nehekharan Undead, Sworn Bodyguard (see page 32).

Settra's Champion: If able to, Nekaph must always issue and accept challenges. When fighting in a challenge, Nekaph gains a 5+ ward save, and his Killing Blow will take effect on any To Wound rolls of 5+.

Herald of Despair: Enemy units in base contact with Nekaph roll one additional dice when taking a Fear test, discarding the lowest result.

MAGIC ITEMS:
Flail of Skulls: *This flail, is made from the gilded skulls of conquered kings, whose skulls bite into their victims.*

Magic Weapon. Requires Two Hands. Attacks made with the Flail of Skulls strike at +2 Strength during the first round of close combat. In addition, the Flail of Skulls has the Multiple Wounds (2) special rule.

"Kneel before the might of Settra the Imperishable, Khemrikhara, King of Nehekhara, Lord of the Earth, Monarch of the Sky, Ruler of the Four Horizons, Mighty Lion of the Infinite Desert, Great Hawk of the Heavens, Majestic Emperor of the Shifting Sands, Eternal Sovereign of Khemri's Legions."

- A small fraction of Nekaph's speech demanding his foe's unconditional surrender.

HIGH QUEEN KHALIDA
BELOVED OF ASAPH

Khalida Neferher, the Warrior-Queen of Lybaras, was highly respected across all the lands of Nehekhara. Her intelligence and bravery were as legendary as her intense sense of honour and justice. Her reign was tragically short, as she was cut down in her prime, and all of Nehekhara mourned her passing.

Khalida was killed by her cousin Neferata, Queen of Lahmia, in ritual combat during a great celebratory feast. Neferata desired the death of Khalida, for the Warrior-Queen had been growing ever more suspicious of her cousin. Khalida was right to be wary, for Neferata had attempted to recreate the Elixir of Life, and in doing so had become the first of the Vampires. If Khalida was not silenced, then the Lahmian's dark secret would be discovered. So it was that Neferata falsely accused Khalida of treason, and the Warrior-Queen rose to personally defend her honour. The two women fought before the shocked nobility, their blades weaving a delicate and deadly dance. Khalida was a skilled warrior, yet she could not match Neferata's preternatural speed or unholy strength and was struck a mortal blow. As Khalida lay dying, Neferata bit hard on her own tongue and placed her mouth over the lips of her cousin, letting vampiric blood flow down the Warrior-Queen's throat. As the life began to leave her body, Khalida knew that cursed blood now flowed through her veins. In desperation, she cried out to the gods to save her from the same fate that had taken hold of Neferata. Asaph, the asp goddess, heard her pleas and purified the vampiric taint from Khalida's veins, though it drained the remaining life from her as well. In sorrow, she was borne back to her home city of Lybaras.

Khalida was embalmed and placed in a seated position within a specially made reliquary. There she sits unmoving, her face concealed behind a beautiful death mask created in her likeness. In times of need Khalida awakens, and the power of Asaph infuses her mummified remains. Her flesh returns to its former beauty, gradually becoming as pale and hard as pristine white marble. Gracefully, she rises from her throne and glides across the temple floor, commanding the tall heavy doors to open with a delicate motion of her hand. Her famed archer legions, buried in vast tomb pits beside the temple, arise at her bidding, marching alongside their immortal Warrior-Queen as they did in life, bringing death to those that intrude upon her realm.

High Queen Khalida is the embodiment of the asp goddess, and divine energy flows through her limbs. Venom runs in Khalida's veins, and she moves with the speed of a striking asp. Only when all her foes lie dead at her feet does she lead her legions back to Lybaras and sit upon her throne again. However, though Khalida sleeps, her soul is troubled. Deep within the High Queen burns a loathing for those tainted by Nagash's vile sorcery, and only when the last Vampire has been slain will she finally rest in peace.

TROOP TYPE: Infantry (Special Character; Tomb King).

SPECIAL RULES: Always Strikes First, The Curse (see page 30), Flammable, Hatred (Vampire Counts), Nehekharan Undead, Poisoned Attacks.

Incarnation of the Asp Goddess: The power of the asp goddess flows in Khalida's veins. Poisoned Attacks cannot wound Khalida automatically – they always roll To Wound.

Blessing of Asaph: The asp goddess smiles on Khalida and her followers. Any unit of Skeleton Archers joined by High Queen Khalida uses her unmodified Ballistic Skill in place of its own. In addition, all shooting attacks made by this unit have the Poisoned Attacks special rule.

MAGIC ITEMS:
The Venom Staff: *Khalida wields a staff shaped like a striking asp that writhes as if alive and spits at its enemies with the anger and spite of Asaph herself.*

Arcane Item. Bound Spell (power level 5). The Venom Staff contains a **magic missile** with a range of 24". If successfully cast, the target takes 2D6 Strength 4 hits.

	M	WS	BS	S	T	W	I	A	LD
High Queen Khalida	6	6	3	4	5	3	9	5	10

GRAND HIEROPHANT KHATEP
LICHE LORD OF KHEMRI

Khatep is the Grand Hierophant of Khemri, the head of the Mortuary Cult's hieratic council, and he alone knows all its secrets and unwritten lore. Khatep is the oldest and wisest of all the Liche Priests and the first member of their order to truly deny death's embrace, if not the ravages of time. He is ancient beyond memory, cadaverous and hunched over as if he carries the weight of epochs upon his shoulders.

Following the casting of Nagash's Great Ritual, civil war threatened to destroy Nehekhara. Khatep therefore took it upon himself to restore order. He broke the magical seals of the Grand Pyramid of Khemri and awoke the greatest of the Tomb Kings – Settra. At the end of the mighty incantation Settra arose and smote any who opposed him. Before long all bowed their heads to Settra, and though he once more sat upon the throne of Khemri, his wrath was great. Settra was angry foremost with the Mortuary Cult, believing they had whispered lies about the extent of their powers. In his fury, he exiled Khatep from Khemri and forbade him to set foot within any of the great cities until such time as he could fulfil the Mortuary Cult's ancient promise and reinstate the golden age of Nehekhara. Thus, Khatep wanders the deserts in search of scrolls, inscriptions and relics of power that he believes will restore his beloved kingdom to its former glory.

Khatep roams the Land of the Dead to this day, lending his aid to the Tomb Kings when he can. When King Dhekesh of Mahrak battled with the Lizardmen of the south, their ferocity proved too great for his skeletal legions. As reptilian soldiers smashed through ranks of Skeletons, and towering war-statues were hewn by powerful magics, Mahrak stood on the brink of destruction. Then, through a whirling cloud of dust a single figure appeared and he intoned a single word that silenced the sorceries of the enemy. This stooped being then raised his copper staff, and across the battlefield the broken bones of thousands of fallen Skeletons were whole again. The Lizardmen found themselves surrounded and outnumbered, and the sands were soon awash with their blood. Before King Dhekesh could greet the mysterious stranger, he had vanished back into the dust-storm. This and a hundred other such tales have been attributed to Grand Hierophant Khatep, the Liche Lord of Khemri.

	M	WS	BS	S	T	W	I	A	LD
Grand Hierophant Khatep	4	3	3	4	3	2	1	9

TROOP TYPE:
Infantry (Special Character; Liche High Priest).

MAGIC:
Grand Hierophant Khatep is a Level 4 Wizard. He uses spells from the Lore of Nehekhara.

SPECIAL RULES: Loremaster (Lore of Nehekhara), Nehekharan Undead.

Grand Hierophant of Khemri: If you take Grand Hierophant Khatep, he must be your army's Hierophant.

MAGIC ITEMS:
The Liche Staff: *This ancient copper staff is inscribed with the names of all the gods and goddesses of Nehekhara and it grants Khatep mastery of their magical power.*

Arcane Item. Khatep can declare that he is using the Liche Staff immediately after rolling the dice to cast a spell, even if the result indicates irresistible force. If Khatep uses the Liche Staff, he re-rolls all the casting dice used in the attempt. Khatep can use the Liche Staff once per turn.

Scroll of the Cursing Word: *This scroll curses those who utter vile sorceries, filling their mouths with dung beetles or replacing the air in their lungs with scorching sand.*

Arcane Item. One Use Only. When an enemy spell has been cast, Khatep can read this scroll instead of attempting to dispel it. The spell is cast as normal, but the caster must immediately take a Toughness test. If the test is passed, nothing happens. If the test is failed, the enemy Wizard cannot cast any more spells that turn, as he spits out a mouthful of foul-tasting insects. If the test is failed on the roll of a 6, the caster immediately suffers D3 Wounds as well, with no saves of any kind allowed.

ARKHAN THE BLACK
THE LICHE KING

Arkhan the Black was the first and most loyal of the evil Nagash's followers. Arkhan helped lead the coup which brought the arch-necromancer to power, and he was the first, after his lord, to imbibe the Elixir of Life. Arkhan was the most adept of Nagash's pupils in the study of dark sorcery, and he quickly rose to become the necromancer's trusted vizier and principal lieutenant. Arkhan led many armies against Nagash's enemies and was never defeated in open combat. In the end, however, the sheer numbers of the Priest Kings' soldiers forced Nagash to retreat. It was Arkhan who led the suicidal counter-attack that gave Nagash the opportunity to escape. For over an hour Arkhan held back the Army of the Seven Kings through feats of martial prowess and powerful sorcery. Arkhan finally fell, not to a hero's sword, but to a single spear hurled by an unknown soldier. Arkhan stared in horror at the shaft protruding from his chest, knowing that it had pierced his heart. With his dying breath, he threatened that a terrible curse would befall any who touched his corpse, and with that, he slumped to the ground. Within seconds, dark flames had consumed Arkhan's flesh leaving behind only a blackened skeleton. Whilst the rest of Nagash's followers were beheaded and burnt, none dared risk desecrating Arkhan's remains, and so they covered them under a cairn of stones instead.

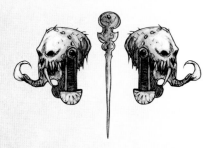

Nagash did not forget his most able lieutenant, and when he returned to wreak vengeance on Nehekhara, Arkhan was reborn as the Liche King – the first of Nagash's nine Dark Lords. These fell beings were the foremost of Nagash's captains, and they brought despair and destruction to his foes. Though Nagash was eventually slain, his loyal servant Arkhan remained. For countless generations, Arkhan the Black vented his anger on the lands of the living, butchering the inhabitants of the world from the kingdoms of Araby in the west to the fledgling Empire in the north. However, Arkhan the Black retained his master's unquenchable thirst for dominion over the realms of Nehekhara above all else, and he finally returned to the Land of the Dead. From his cursed Black Tower, Arkhan has carved out a powerful realm. The other Tomb Kings tolerate Arkhan, for he is a powerful ally to those who can afford his price.

Of all the rulers in the Land of the Dead, Arkhan's greatest rival remains Settra the Imperishable. The two have fought against each other a dozen times, and though Arkhan's army cannot rival the might of Settra's, neither can the King of Nehekhara overcome the Liche King's dark sorcery. Their battles thus end in stalemate, and only when Arkhan bows

his head and utters false promises of fealty does Settra return satisfied to Khemri. Whilst Arkhan feigns servitude, he is secretly plotting for a way to hasten the inevitable return of Nagash. To this end, he has scoured the globe in search of the Great Necromancer's enchanted items, for a fraction of his evil will still resides within each. Arkhan the Black wields his master's own magical staff, plucked from the clutches of the Vampire Mandregan, and with it he channels the Winds of Magic to his whim. However, Arkhan's most prized possession is the Liber Mortis, one of the nine Books of Nagash that hold the secrets to necromantic magic. One day Arkhan the Black will succeed in resurrecting his dark master, and on that day the Tomb Kings shall be destroyed, and the world shall drown in death.

	M	WS	BS	S	T	W	I	A	LD
Arkhan the Black	4	4	3	5	5	3	3	3	9

TROOP TYPE: Infantry (Special Character; Liche High Priest & Tomb King).

MAGIC: Arkhan is a Level 4 Wizard. He uses spells from the Lore of Death, even if he is your army's Hierophant.

SPECIAL RULES: The Curse (see page 30), Nehekharan Undead, Flammable.

MAGIC ITEMS:

The Tomb Blade of Arkhan: *The flesh of those slain by this dread blade burns away, leaving behind only a charred skeleton enslaved for all eternity to Arkhan's dark will.*

Magic Weapon. For every unsaved Wound caused by this blade to an enemy in close combat, Arkhan's unit immediately recovers a Wound for each one inflicted, as described in Resurrecting Fallen Warriors (see page 28).

Staff of Nagash: *This staff was created by the Arch Necromancer Nagash to harness the reservoirs of dark magic stored within the accursed Black Pyramid.*

Arcane Item. At the end of the opponent's Magic phase, you can store up to three unused dispel dice from your pool in the Staff of Nagash. At the beginning of your next Magic phase, add these dice to your power dice pool. If Arkhan the Black is removed as a casualty before your next Magic phase, these power dice are lost.

The Liber Mortis: *This accursed tome is one of the fabled nine Books of Nagash, the most potent source of necromantic magic in the world.*

Arcane Item. Whilst Arkhan the Black has the Liber Mortis his Wizard Level is increased to 5. If the Liber Mortis is ever destroyed, Arkhan the Black immediately loses a Wizard Level, and therefore must lose a randomly determined spell.

PRINCE APOPHAS
THE CURSED SCARAB LORD

Apophas was a jealous prince who lusted after the throne of Numas. To this end, he slit the throats of the entire royal line while they slept and proclaimed himself king. However, the people of Numas rebelled against him, and those loyal to the murdered king broke into the throne room and dragged the usurper to the temples to be judged. Of all the crimes in Nehekhara, the most terrible was regicide. Typically, those who attempted to seize the throne were denied the privilege of mummification, and their bones were thrown to the carrion of the desert. Denied access to the lands of the honoured dead, these unfortunates were consigned, at best, to the torturous depths of the Nehekharan Underworld, or at worst, to utter oblivion. Apophas' crimes warranted a more severe punishment; he was entombed alive within a sarcophagus filled with flesh-eating scarabs. It is said that his death screams could be heard through the temple walls, but when the lid was opened, there was no trace of the beetles. All that remained was a skull picked clean of flesh. Before this was thrown into the deep desert, it was inscribed with a single magical hieroglyph cursing Apophas' soul for all eternity.

Upon his death, Apophas' soul was claimed by Usirian, god of the Underworld, to be tormented in perpetuity for his crimes. However, being of noble birth, Apophas was able to strike a bargain with Usirian, promising that, in exchange for his release, he would claim for the god a soul to stand in his stead, a perfect match for his own. Usirian agreed, and thus Apophas was reborn as the Cursed Scarab Lord.

Apophas appears from a swarm of beetles that flow up from the ground until they reveal a black-swathed figure in their midst. Apophas is not a reanimated corpse but a desert-revenant whose body is formed from a writhing swarm of scarabs. Atop this undulating mass, his skull looks upon the world in search of his chosen victim – a soul he believes can buy his freedom. In Apophas' hand is the same blade he used to slit the throats of his family, and it drips with their blood to this day. Only by slaying the perfect soul with this weapon can Apophas hope to earn his freedom.

The scarabs making up Apophas' form scuttle over rubble and through gaps in ruins without impediment. Apophas' body can even burst apart in an explosion of chitinous wings, flying across the battlefield before reforming into the mocking semblance of a man. Apophas sweeps aside those that stand between him and his prey, and when he opens his jaw, a tide of insects erupts forth to drown his foes. No matter how hard his enemies swipe and hack at his horrifying form, insect bodies flow over to fill open wounds and re-grow lost limbs. Apophas is utterly implacable, and he will not stop until his victim lies dead at his hand.

Apophas then binds his target's spirit in a mystical soul-cage before returning to the depths of the Underworld. Here the soul is placed on a pair of scales and compared with Apophas' own cursed spirit. However, the truth is that no two souls are ever equal, and the scales are never balanced. Though he doesn't know it, Apophas has doomed himself to roam the lands for eternity.

	M	WS	BS	S	T	W	I	A	LD
Prince Apophas	4	4	3	4	3	4	1	5	8

UNIT TYPE: Infantry (Special Character; Tomb Prince).

SPECIAL RULES: Entombed Beneath the Sands, Fly, Nehekharan Undead, Regeneration, Strider, Terror.

Desert Revenant: Prince Apophas cannot join any units, and he cannot be your army's General.

Scarab Prince: Prince Apophas' body is made of a scuttling tide of scarabs that he can vomit over his foes. Apophas has a Strength 2 Breath Weapon. In addition, if Apophas is ever destroyed (by any means), then before removing the model all enemy units within 2D6" of him immediately take 2D6 Strength 2 hits, distributed as for shooting.

Soul Reaper: As soon as Prince Apophas is placed on the tabletop, nominate one enemy character on the battlefield – this is the soul marked by the god of the Underworld that Apophas must claim. Apophas re-rolls any failed To Hit and To Wound rolls against the chosen character.

RAMHOTEP THE VISIONARY
NECROTECT OF QUATAR

Ramhotep the Visionary was perhaps the greatest Necrotect in history. His craftsmanship was second to none, and it is said that his statues in the Valley of Kings were so lifelike that the kings of Nehekhara believed the gods themselves had returned to the mortal world. He designed the Grand Necropolis of Rasetra, the Monuments of Eternal Death in Zandri, the Monoliths of the Great Plains and many other architectural wonders. However, Ramhotep took credit for not one of these grand monuments, for to do so would have been tantamount to signing his own death warrant.

In ancient Nehekhara, the finest artisans were commissioned to build grand burial tombs and upon completion they were expected to commit ritual suicide. Ramhotep was aghast at the thought, for it would deny the world of the beautiful creations he had yet to make. Thus, Ramhotep would manipulate the more arrogant Necrotects of the age to take his place. Ramhotep posed as an eager student to the renowned Ramakat the Creative, as a pupil to Emrah the Artisan, and as an assistant to a dozen other legendary architects. These great artisans were stricken with blood-lotus addiction shortly afterwards, consumed in a drug-addled stupor as Ramhotep crafted a mask in their image – one so perfect that none could tell the difference. Ramhotep assumed their identities and oversaw the construction of many magnificent monuments. Each time, shortly before the project's completion, he disappeared and a very confused Necrotect was sacrificed and interred within the tomb in Ramhotep's stead. It is said that they protested loudly – but these were dismissed as the ravings of a mad artist.

Inlife, Ramhotep was consumed by a frenzied compulsion to create and build. No matter how quickly his underlings accomplished their tasks, it was not fast enough for Ramhotep, for there were always more ambitious and grander projects that needed his attention. However, Ramhotep's vision reached past his mortal lifespan, and as he withered in old age, he realised that the only way he could finish his work was if he was granted the honour of mummification. Thus, after several decades of careful anonymity, Ramhotep removed his mask and agreed to build a pyramid that would rival the majesty of the Great Pyramid of Khemri. Thousands of work gangs slaved and died under the desert sun to build the Sepulchre of the Heavens in Quatar, and none dared slacken their pace in his presence, for Ramhotep was quick with the lash and would dole out fierce punishments to those who would jeopardise his art. In his final days, before the last cornerstone was heaved into position, Ramhotep fashioned for himself a death mask and prepared himself for his interment. The king of Quatar was mightily pleased with his tomb and rewarded Ramhotep with an exquisite burial ceremony. For countless centuries afterwards, the artisan's corpse rested within his splendid monument.

Few of Ramhotep's works have endured unscathed through the ages. Half of his creations lie forgotten beneath the sands, and those that have remained have been battered by centuries of war and eroded by time and sandstorms. Upon awakening from his death sleep, Ramhotep was horrified, and he set about excavating and restoring his marvels at once. Ramhotep's skill in undeath is as great as it was in life, and the statues that receive his attentions are restored to their former majesty, striding into battle as if they were carved only yesterday. He works relentlessly to maintain his masterpieces, and such is the likeness between these effigies and the gods they represent, that the ancient pantheon blesses them and protects them in battle. With this army of walking statues, Ramhotep intends to pull down the cities of those who defiled his work, slay the inhabitants of these uncultured civilisations, and construct his greatest monument to date: a vast mausoleum built from the bones of his foes. Those who stand in his way feel the lash of Ramhotep's whip, and their flesh parts from their bones as the ancient architect vents his frustration and anger.

	M	WS	BS	S	T	W	I	A	LD
Ramhotep the Visionary	4	3	3	4	4	2	3	2	7

UNIT TYPE: Infantry (Special Character; Necrotect).

SPECIAL RULES: Flammable, Frenzy, Hatred, Nehekharan Undead, Stone Shaper (see page 33), Wrath of the Creator (see page 33).

Frantic Fervour: Ramhotep confers the Frenzy special rule onto the unit he accompanies. If he leaves the unit, or is slain, the unit immediately loses Frenzy.

Master Artisan: At the start of the game, randomly select a single friendly unit that has the Animated Construct rule. The Animated Constructs in this unit have been restored and embellished by Ramhotep, and re-roll all failed armour saves during the battle.

RAMHOTEP'S REVENGE

When an Empire army from Reikland invaded Quatar in the Imperial year 2141, they damaged dozens of Ramhotep's works as they looted the city's tombs. This desecration was bad enough, but when the Steam Tank Deliverance smashed through Ramhotep's Terracotta Wall, the Necrotect entered a fit of apopleptic rage, and he swore he would have his revenge. Ramhotep worked for over a century to complete the restoration of his Marble Army, an awe-inspiring host of hundreds of towering constructs. Such was the demented architect's need for vengeance that, in exchange for eight jade Warsphinxes, he enlisted the aid of Arkhan the Black, who raised a mighty bridge of bones through dark sorcery to span the Black Mountains. Ramhotep's statuesque army marched across, and the cities of Übersreik and Grünburg were all but destroyed, despite the fact that every soldier to have been involved in the destruction of his precious masterpiece had been dead for at least 170 years.

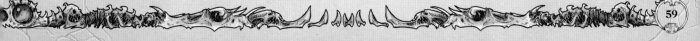

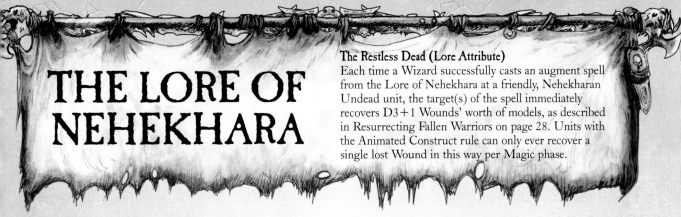

THE LORE OF NEHEKHARA

Khsar's Incantation of the Desert Wind (Signature Spell)   Cast on 8+

Harnessing the power of Khsar, god of the desert winds, the Liche Priest summons forth a sandstorm that engulfs the undying warriors of Nehekhara and carries them across the battlefield.

Khsar's Incantation of the Desert Wind is an **augment** spell that targets all unengaged friendly Nehekharan Undead units within 12". The targets can immediately make a normal move as if it were the Remaining Moves sub-phase. The Wizard can choose to have this spell target all unengaged friendly Nehekharan Undead units within 24". If he does so, the casting value is increased to 16+. No unit can be moved by *Khsar's Incantation of the Desert Wind* more than once per turn (though they still benefit from the Restless Dead Lore Attribute).

1. Djaf's Incantation of Cursed Blades   Cast on 7+

As the Liche Priest utters this ancient mantra, he imbues the weapons of the Nehekharan warriors with the essence of Djaf, the jackal-headed god of the dead, who hungers for the souls of the living above all things.

Djaf's Incantation of Cursed Blades is an **augment** spell with a range of 12". The target unit's close combat Attacks gain the Killing Blow ability until the start of your next Magic phase. If the target unit's Attacks already have the Killing Blow or Heroic Killing Blow ability, these will take effect on any To Wound rolls of a 5 or 6 whilst this spell is in play. The Wizard can choose to extend the range of this spell to 24". If he does so, the casting value is increased to 10+.

2. Neru's Incantation of Protection   Cast on 9+

As the Liche Priest intones this blessing, his foes find their sword strokes mysteriously turned aside as Neru, wife of Ptra and goddess of protection, reaches out to shield Nehekhara's warriors from the evils of the night.

Neru's Incantation of Protection is an **augment** spell with a range of 12". The target unit gains a 5+ ward save until the start of the caster's next Magic phase. The Wizard can instead choose to have this spell target all friendly Nehekharan Undead units within 12". If he does so, the casting value is increased to 18+.

3. Ptra's Incantation of Righteous Smiting   Cast on 9+

As the verses of this incantation are spoken, a fierce light emanates from the empty eye sockets of the Nehekharan Undead as the power of Ptra infuses these warriors with the speed and fury to smite their foes.

Ptra's Incantation of Righteous Smiting is an **augment** spell with a range of 12". The target's Attacks are increased by 1 until the start of the caster's next Magic phase (this includes the Attacks of mounts and models crewing a war machine, chariot, monster etc). In addition, if the target unit is armed with a bow or great bow, it gains the Multiple Shot (2) special rule until the start of the caster's next Magic phase.

The Wizard can instead choose to have this spell target all friendly Nehekharan Undead units within 24". If he does so, the casting value is increased to 18+.

4. Usirian's Incantation of Vengeance   Cast on 10+

Skeletal hands burst from beneath the surface to drag those above into a grave as the Liche Priest invokes the names of Usirian.

Usirian's Incantation of Vengeance is a **hex** spell with a range of 18". The target unit suffers -D3 to its Movement (to a minimum of 1) and treats all terrain (even open ground) as Dangerous Terrain, testing every time it moves (including when charging, fleeing, pursuing, moving compulsorily, etc.) until the start of the caster's next Magic phase. The Wizard can instead choose to extend the range of this spell to 36". If he does so, the casting value is increased to 13+.

5. Usekhp's Incantation of Desiccation   Cast on 11+

As the Liche Priest intones the curse of desiccation, every syllable strips the moisture from his victims' bodies, sapping their vitality.

Usekhp's Incantation of Desiccation is a **hex** spell with a range of 24". The target unit has -1 Strength and -1 Toughness (to a minimum of 1) until the start of the caster's next Magic phase. The Wizard can choose to reduce the target's Strength and Toughness by D3 (to a minimum of 1) until the start of his next Magic phase. If he does so, the casting value is increased to 22+.

6. Sakhmet's Incantation of the Skullstorm   Cast on 15+

A whirlwind of skulls tears across the battlefield, devouring everything in its path in the name of the goddess Sakhmet.

Remains in play. *Sakhmet's Incantation of the Skullstorm* is a **magical vortex** that uses the small round template. Once the template is placed, the player nominates the direction in which the Skullstorm will move. To determine how many inches the template moves, roll an artillery dice and multiply the result by the caster's Wizard level. If the result on the artillery dice is a misfire, centre the template on the caster instead; the template moves a number of inches equal to the caster's Wizard level, in a random direction (if you roll a hit, the template remains where it is). Any model under, or passed over by, the template suffers a single Strength 4 hit. In subsequent turns, the Skullstorm travels in a random direction and moves a number of inches equal to the roll of an artillery dice (if a misfire is rolled, the Skullstorm dissipates and is removed). A Wizard can infuse the Skullstorm with more power, so that it uses the large round template instead. If he does so, the casting value is increased to 25+.

TREASURES OF THE NECROPOLIS

On the following pages are magic items available to Tomb Kings armies. These can be taken in addition to any of the magic items listed in the Warhammer rulebook.

DESTROYER OF ETERNITIES   80 points
Magic Weapon

The bloodthirsty King Nekhesh was the first to wield this massive, ornate blade in battle, severing limbs and heads with every sweeping blow. Imbued with powerful incantations, the blade of this weapon is impossibly sharp and can cleave through armour, flesh and bone with equal ease. Furthermore, this weapon is said to destroy the souls of its victims, thereby denying them any hope of reaching the afterlife. The Destroyer of Eternities was thus greatly feared in ancient Nehekhara, and to be slain by its cursed blade was considered a fate infinitely worse than mere death.

Tomb King on foot only. Attacks made with the Destroyer of Eternities are at +2 Strength, and have the Heroic Killing Blow special rule. The wielder can choose to exchange all of his Attacks to make a special 'Sweeping Attack' – if he does so, all enemy models in base contact with the wielder suffer a single automatic hit (also at +2 Strength and with Heroic Killing Blow). If a target is a character riding a chariot or monster, then both the rider and mount each take a single automatic hit. In a challenge, only the models engaged in the challenge count as being in base contact with the Tomb King.

BLADE OF ANTARHAK   50 points
Magic Weapon

Forged for the Tomb Prince Antarhak, this weapon draws the life energy from the slain and suffuses the wielder with the stolen essence. Those whose bodies are pierced by this cursed blade age decades in mere seconds, their once powerful frames reduced to withered husks in the span of a few heartbeats. As the foe's vitality is sapped, the wielder's wounds heal, and a semblance of youth returns, if only temporarily, to their time-ravaged features.

For every unsaved Wound inflicted by the Blade of Antarhak, the wielder immediately regains a single Wound lost earlier in the battle. If the bearer is already at his starting number of Wounds and inflicts another unsaved Wound with this weapon, he gains the Regeneration special rule until the end of the next player turn.

GOLDEN DEATH MASK OF KHARNUT   60 points
Enchanted Item

According to Nehekharan beliefs, in the afterlife the gods would bestow each king with a body of gold. Thus, when Prince Kharnut awoke from his death-sleep he was horrified at his withered, skeletal visage and demanded the Mortuary Cult fashion for him a magnificent golden death mask. However, when the mask was being sealed around Kharnut's head, a drop of molten gold fell upon the Prince's embalmed body, immolating him in a fiery blaze. The Prince's spirit was not destroyed, but was mystically bound within the expressionless mask. The taint of death hangs heavy upon the death mask, gripping the hearts of all who gaze upon it.

The model wearing this mask causes Terror. In addition, enemy units within 6" of the wearer cannot make use of their general's Inspiring Presence special rule or their Battle Standard Bearer's Hold Your Ground special rule.

CLOAK OF THE DUNES   50 points
Enchanted Item

This fabled cloak is said to have been created by Khsar the Faceless, the god of the desert who took on the form on the elemental wind. The Cloak of the Dunes is infused with the magic of the deserts, enabling the wearer to transform himself into a whirling cloud of sand. As the bearer moves across the desert, a cone of sharp sand follows in his wake that can strip flesh from bone.

Infantry character on foot only. The wearer of the Cloak of Dunes has the Fly special rule. In addition, if the bearer moves over an unengaged enemy unit in the Remaining Moves sub-phase, that enemy unit immediately suffers 2D6 Strength 2 hits, resolved as for shooting attacks. The bearer can move over several enemy units in the same turn if you wish, causing damage to every unit. The same target unit cannot be affected more than once in the same turn.

NEFERRA'S SCROLLS OF MIGHTY INCANTATIONS
Arcane Item   50 points

Neferra, High Priestess to King Khutef, committed her lifetime of knowledge to eight enchanted scrolls so that it would never be lost. The ink with which the hieroglyphs were inscribed was mixed with the blood of sacrificed slaves, each drop being individually blessed in a week-long ritual. Each scroll took over a decade of painstaking work to complete, but the raw power imbued within them can transform the simplest incantation into an unstoppable hurricane of power. Neferra was so paranoid that a rival might steal her sacred scrolls that she also wrought powerful curses onto the parchments that would bring about an unwitting thief's destruction.

One use only. A Wizard can declare that he is using Neferra's Scrolls of Mighty Incantations immediately before casting a spell. If he does so, the Wizard must add a number of extra bonus dice, equal to his Wizard level, to the power dice he is going to roll (you still need to roll at least one dice from the power pool). The bonus dice do not count as power dice. However, a roll of any double when casting a spell using them will cause irresistible force (and a miscast).

ENKHIL'S KANOPI
Arcane Item   25 points

Within this inauspicious clay vessel is the ancient heart of High Priest Enkhil, removed from his corpse when he was embalmed and entombed within the great necropolis of Mahrak. Enkhil was a jealous and powerful priest, and his undying essence is contained within his shrivelled heart to this day. When the vulture-headed lid is opened, this canopic jar sucks the swirling magical energy from the air, drawing the power into the vessel itself. Enkhil's Kanopi is much sought after, as it can not only thwart the sorceries of enemy wizards, but also strengthen a Liche Priest's own incantations.

Bound spell (Power Level 3). If cast successfully, roll a D6 for every 'remains in play' spell on the tabletop: on a 2+ that spell is automatically dispelled. For each spell that is ended in this way, add D3 power dice to your power pool.

STANDARD OF THE UNDYING LEGION
Magic Standard   50 points

This great standard once decorated the tomb of King Lahmizzar's Jackal Legion, the elite Tomb Guard of Quatar. Every one of these warriors, the fiercest of all the king's army, swore their oath of eternal servitude under the shadow of this banner, slitting their palms and daubing the standard's top – a likeness of Djaf, the jackal-headed god of the dead – in their own blood. The spirits of Lahmizzar's legion live on within this ancient icon to this day. Whenever the Standard of the Undying Legion is taken forth into battle, these warrior-spirits restore the fallen and inhabit their bodies to fight again and fulfil their undying pledge.

Bound Spell (power level 5). This banner contains an **augment** spell that can only be cast on the bearer's unit. If successfully cast, the bearer's unit immediately recovers D6+2 Wounds' worth of models, as described in Resurrecting Fallen Warriors on page 28.

BANNER OF THE HIDDEN DEAD
Magic Standard   90 points

Belonging to the fabled Hawk Legion, the elite army who guarded Settra before his mummification, the Banner of the Hidden Dead summons the souls of one of their regiments from their honoured place in the Underworld. Wrought with powerful incantations, the ancient dead are called to this banner like moths to a flame. The magic of the banner then binds these souls into the skeletal remains of warriors who have long lain buried and forgotten beneath the sands. At a wordless command, skeletal soldiers punch through the desert surface, forming into perfect ranks or long-dead charioteers burst forth from the dunes for the first time in millenia, ready to wage war once more for the glory of Nehekhara.

Nominate one of your units of infantry, cavalry, or chariots with the Nehekharan Undead rule that has yet to deploy, whose total points value is no greater than 150 points. That unit gains the Entombed Beneath the Sands special rule (see page 29). When this unit arrives on the battlefield you must place its 'Entombed Beneath the Sands' marker within 12" of the Banner of the Hidden Dead. If the bearer of this banner is destroyed before the hidden unit emerges, the entire hidden unit is destroyed and removed as casualties.

In addition, every unit with the Entombed Beneath the Sands special rule that attempts to emerge whilst its marker is within 12" of the Banner of the Hidden Dead (including your nominated hidden unit) can re-roll the scatter and artillery dice when emerging. Note that you must either re-roll both, or neither of the dice.

THE DEAD AWAKEN

A well-painted army arrayed for battle on the tabletop is an inspirational sight for any Warhammer hobbyist. Those looking to raise their own Tomb Kings force, or add to their existing collection, have a diverse range of models to choose from and countless thousands of ways to forge them into an army. A Tomb Kings commander can grind his foes to nothing in battles of attrition with huge legions of skeletal infantry, sweep his enemies from the battlefield with regiments of chariots, or crush them to dust with giant, stone monsters.

This section presents a showcase of some of the fantastic Citadel miniatures available to the Tomb Kings. It is a glorious guide that will inspire collectors, painters and wargamers alike.

Tomb Herald Battle Standard Bearer.

Prince Apophas.

Liche Priest on Skeletal Steed.

Necrotect.

Tomb King.

High Queen Khalida.

Settra the Imperishable on the Chariot of the Gods.

A regiment of Tomb Guard.

Tomb Guard bear the insignia and colours of their king.

A regiment of Skeleton Warriors.

Skeleton Warriors of the Crimson King of Numas.

Skeleton Warriors. *Skeleton Archers.*

A regiment of Skeleton Archers.

Implacable phalanxes of Skeletons stand ready to defend their Tomb King's realm.

A regiment of Skeleton Horsemen patrolling the necropolises of Nehekhara.

Skeleton Horse Archer.

Skeleton Horseman.

Skeleton Horse Archers.

Skeleton Horseman.

Tomb King on Skeleton Chariot.

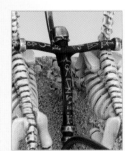

Skeleton Chariot.

The Tomb Kings maintain vast legions of Skeleton Chariots.

Necropolis Knights spearhead a Tomb King army's attack.

Necropolis Knights.

Necropolis Knights ride to war atop monstrous Necroserpents.

Carrion advance in the wake of a Tomb Guard and Tomb Swarm attack.

Ushabti with great bows.

Ushabti are animated statues carved in the likeness of ancient Nehekharan gods.

A monstrous regiment of Ushabti awaken to smite their Tomb King's enemies.

A Casket of Souls and Screaming Skull Catapults unleash a barrage of death at their foes.

Tomb Scorpion.

Casket of Souls.

Necrosphinx.

Tomb King.

A Khemrian Warsphinx, crewed by elite Tomb Guard warriors.

Khemrian Warsphinx ridden by a Tomb King.

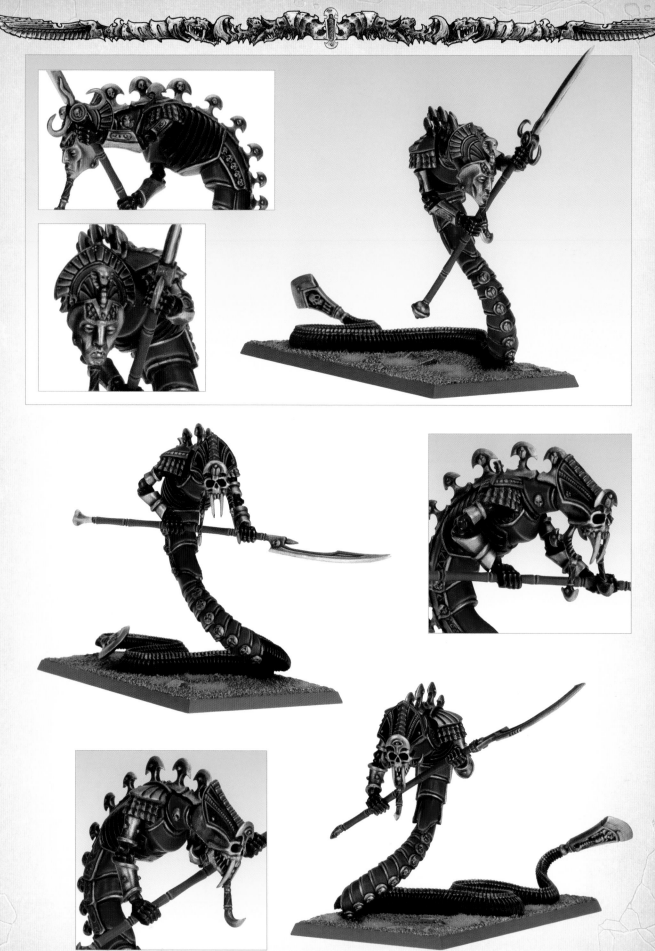

Sepulchral Stalkers.

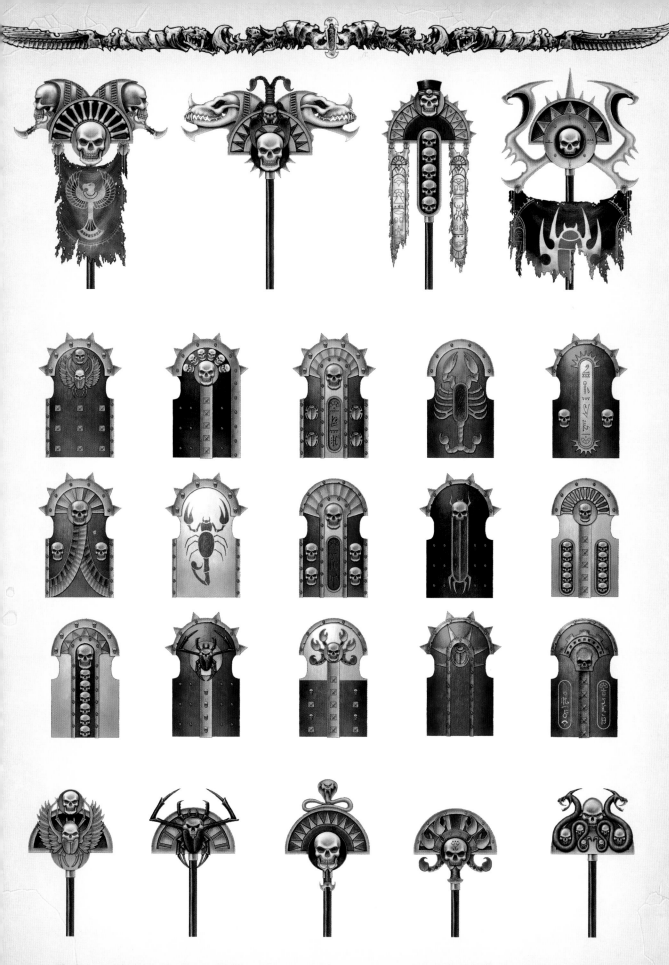

The legions of the Tomb Kings carry shields and banners displaying the dynastic colours and symbols of their Undead monarchs.

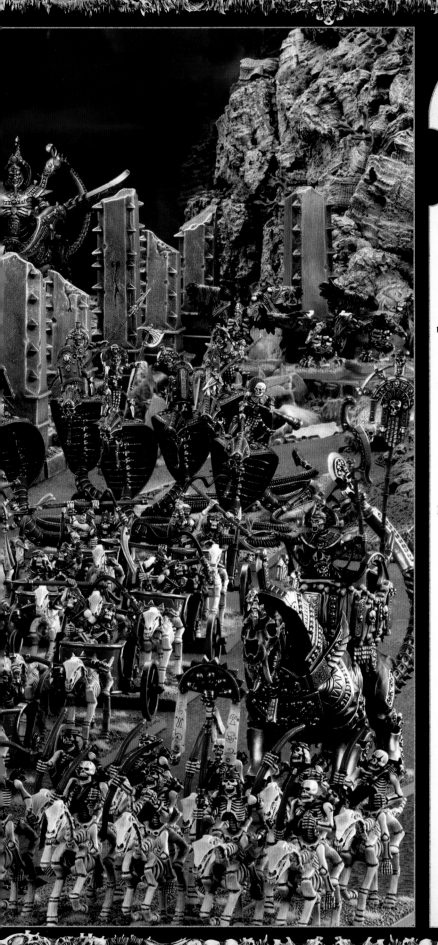

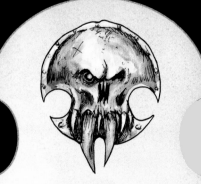

TOMB KINGS ARMY LIST

The immortal Tomb Kings are driven by an unquenchable need to conquer their enemies and reclaim their former realms. As a commander of a Tomb Kings army, it is by your will that the Undead legions of Nehekhara awaken from their slumber of death and stride into battle once more.

This section of the book helps you to turn your collection of Tomb Kings Citadel miniatures into a legion of Undead soldiers ready for a tabletop battle. At the back of this section, you will also find a summary page, which lists every unit's characteristics profile, for quick and easy reference during your games.

USING THE ARMY LIST

The army list is used alongside the 'Choosing an Army' section of the Warhammer rulebook to pick a force ready for battle. Over the following pages you will find an entry for each of the models in your army. These entries give you all of the gaming information that you need to shape your collection of models into the units that will form your army. Amongst other things, they will tell you what your models are equipped with, what options are available to them, and their points costs.

UNIT CATEGORIES

As described in the Warhammer rulebook, the units in the army list are organised into five categories: Lords, Heroes, Core Units, Special Units and Rare Units.

ARMY LIST ENTRIES

Each army list entry contains all the information you need to choose and field that unit at a glance, using the following format:

① **SKELETON WARRIORS**   ④ **4 points per model**

Profile ②	M	WS	BS	S	T	W	I	A	Ld	③ Troop Type
Skeleton Warrior	4	2	2	3	3	1	2	1	5	Infantry
Master of Arms	4	2	2	3	3	1	2	2	5	Infantry

⑤ **Unit Size:** 10+

⑥ **Equipment:**
- Hand weapon
- Shield

⑦ **Special Rules:**
- Nehekharan Undead

⑧ **Options:**
- May upgrade one Skeleton Warrior to a Master of Arms . . . . *10 points*
- May upgrade one Skeleton Warrior to a musician . . . . *10 points*
- May upgrade one Skeleton Warrior to a standard bearer . . . . *10 points*
- The entire unit may take any of the following:
  - Spears . . . . *1 point per model*
  - Light armour . . . . *1 point per model*

① **Name.** *The name by which the unit or character is identified.*

② **Profiles.** *The characteristic profiles for the model(s) in each unit are provided as a reminder. Where several profiles are required, these are also given, even if they are optional (such as unit champions, for example).*

③ **Troop Type.** *Each entry specifies the unit type of its models (e.g. 'infantry', 'cavalry' and so on).*

④ **Points Value.** *Every miniature in the Warhammer range costs an amount of points that reflects how effective it is on the battlefield. For example, a Skeleton Warrior costs 4 points, while the mighty Settra costs 475 points!*

⑤ **Unit Size.** *This specifies the minimum size for each unit, which is the smallest number of models needed to form that unit. In some cases units also have a maximum size, or can even comprise just a single model.*

⑥ **Equipment.** *This is a list of the standard weapons and armour for that unit. The cost of these items is included in the basic points value.*

⑦ **Special Rules.** *Many troops have special rules that are fully described earlier in this book or in the Warhammer rulebook. The names of these rules are listed here as a reminder.*

⑧ **Options.** *A list of optional weapons and armour, mounts, magic items and other upgrades for units or characters, including the points cost for each particular option. Many unit entries include the option to upgrade a unit member to a champion, standard bearer or musician. Some units may carry a magic banner or take magic items at a further points cost.*

The Skeleton Warrior on the left is armed with a spear and a shield. As you can see from the profile above, he will cost 5 points to include in your army. A unit of ten skeletons armed like this would therefore cost 50 points.

The Skeleton Warrior on the left is armed with a hand weapon and a shield, and he costs 4 points. The Skeleton on the right is a Master of Arms. To upgrade a Skeleton Warrior unit to include this champion will cost you an additional 10 points.

LORDS

SETTRA THE IMPERISHABLE
475 points

Profile	M	WS	BS	S	T	W	I	A	Ld	Troop Type
Settra the Imperishable	4	7	3	6	5	4	3	5	10	Infantry (Special Character; Tomb King & Liche Priest)
Chariot of the Gods	-	-	-	5	5	5	-	-	-	Chariot (Armour Save 4+)
Skeletal Steed	8	2	-	3	-	-	2	1	-	

Magic:
Settra is a Level 1 Wizard. He uses spells from the Lore of Nehekhara.

Equipment:
- The Blessed Blade of Ptra
- Light armour
- Chariot of the Gods
- The Crown of Nehekhara
- The Scarab Brooch of Usirian

Special Rules:
- The Curse
- Flammable
- My Will Be Done
- Nehekharan Undead
- Settra the Great

Settra the Imperishable may be your army's Hierophant, as detailed on page 28.

HIGH QUEEN KHALIDA
365 points

Profile	M	WS	BS	S	T	W	I	A	Ld	Troop Type
High Queen Khalida	6	6	3	4	5	3	9	5	10	Infantry (Special Character; Tomb King)

Equipment:
- The Venom Staff
- Light armour

Special Rules:
- Always Strikes First
- Blessing of Asaph
- The Curse
- Flammable
- Hatred (Vampire Counts)
- Incarnation of the Asp Goddess
- Nehekharan Undead
- Poisoned Attacks

ARKHAN THE BLACK
360 points

Profile	M	WS	BS	S	T	W	I	A	Ld	Troop Type
Arkhan the Black	4	4	3	5	5	3	3	3	9	Infantry (Special Character; Liche High Priest & Tomb King)

Magic:
Arkhan the Black is a Level 4 Wizard. He uses spells from the Lore of Death.

Equipment:
- The Tomb Blade of Arkhan
- Light armour
- The Liber Mortis
- The Staff of Nagash

Special Rules:
- The Curse
- Flammable
- Nehekharan Undead

Options:
- May be mounted on a Skeleton Chariot
  (See page 91 for profile. Count the cost of the chariot against your
  allowance for Lords. Arkhan replaces the chariot's crew) ....55 *points*
- May upgrade chariot to have 2 additional Skeletal Steeds.................15 *points*
- May upgrade chariot to have the Fly special rule...........................30 *points*

Arkhan the Black may be your army's Hierophant, as detailed on page 28.

LORDS

GRAND HIEROPHANT KHATEP — 330 points

Profile	M	WS	BS	S	T	W	I	A	Ld	Troop Type
Grand Hierophant Khatep	4	3	3	3	4	3	2	1	9	Infantry (Special Character; Liche High Priest)

Magic:
Grand Hierophant Khatep is a Level 4 Wizard. He uses spells from the Lore of Nehekhara.

Equipment:
- Hand weapon
- The Liche Staff
- Scroll of the Cursing Word

Special Rules:
- Grand Hierophant of Khemri*
- Loremaster (Lore of Nehekhara)
- Nehekharan Undead

* If Grand Hierophant Khatep is in your army, he must be the Hierophant, as detailed on page 28.

TOMB KING — 170 points

Profile	M	WS	BS	S	T	W	I	A	Ld	Troop Type
Tomb King	4	6	3	5	5	4	3	4	10	Infantry (Character)

Equipment:
- Hand weapon
- Light armour

Special Rules:
- The Curse
- Flammable
- My Will Be Done
- Nehekharan Undead

Options:
- May be armed with one of the following:
  - Great weapon .... 6 points
  - Flail .... 6 points
  - Spear .... 3 points
- May take a shield .... 3 points
- May be mounted on one of the following:
  - Skeleton Chariot (See page 91 for profile. Count the cost against your allowance for Lords. The Tomb King replaces the chariot's crew) .... 55 points
  - Khemrian Warsphinx (See page 93 for points and options. Count the cost against your allowance for Lords. The Tomb King replaces the Warsphinx's crew) .... 210 points
- May take magic items up to a total of .... 100 points

LICHE HIGH PRIEST — 175 points

Profile	M	WS	BS	S	T	W	I	A	Ld	Troop Type
Liche High Priest	4	3	3	3	4	3	2	1	8	Infantry (Character)

Magic:
A Liche High Priest is a Level 3 Wizard.
He may use spells from one of the following:
- the Lore of Nehekhara
- the Lore of Light
- the Lore of Death

Equipment:
- Hand weapon

Special Rules:
- Nehekharan Undead

Options:
- May upgrade to a Level 4 Wizard .... 35 points
- May be mounted on a Skeletal Steed .... 15 points
- May take magic items up to a total of .... 100 points

A Liche High Priest may be your army's Hierophant, as detailed on page 28.

HEROES

THE HERALD NEKAPH — 120 points

Profile	M	WS	BS	S	T	W	I	A	Ld	Troop Type
The Herald Nekaph	4	5	3	4	4	2	3	3	8	Infantry (Special Character; Tomb Herald)

Equipment:
- Flail of Skulls
- Light armour

Special Rules:
- Flammable
- Herald of Despair
- Killing Blow
- Nehekharan Undead
- Sworn Bodyguard
- Settra's Champion

Options:
- May be mounted on one of the following:
  - Skeleton Chariot (See page 91 for profile. Count the cost of the chariot against your allowance for Heroes. Nekaph replaces the chariot's crew)........55 points
  - Skeletal Steed...10 points

PRINCE APOPHAS — 130 points

Profile	M	WS	BS	S	T	W	I	A	Ld	Troop Type
Prince Apophas	4	4	3	4	3	4	1	5	8	Infantry (Special Character; Tomb Prince)

Equipment:
- Hand weapon
- Light armour

Special Rules:
- Desert Revenant
- Entombed Beneath the Sands
- Fly
- Nehekharan Undead
- Regeneration
- Scarab Prince
- Soul Reaper
- Strider
- Terror

RAMHOTEP THE VISIONARY — 110 points

Profile	M	WS	BS	S	T	W	I	A	Ld	Troop Type
Ramhotep the Visionary	4	3	3	4	4	2	3	2	7	Infantry (Special Character; Necrotect)

Equipment:
- Hand weapon
- Whip (additional hand weapon)
- Light armour

Special Rules:
- Flammable
- Frantic Fervour
- Master Artisan
- Frenzy
- Nehekharan Undead
- Stone Shaper
- Wrath of the Creator
- Hatred

TOMB PRINCE — 100 points

Profile	M	WS	BS	S	T	W	I	A	Ld	Troop Type
Tomb Prince	4	5	3	4	5	3	3	3	9	Infantry (Character)

Equipment:
- Hand weapon
- Light armour

Special Rules:
- The Curse
- Flammable
- My Will Be Done
- Nehekharan Undead

Options:
- May be armed with one of the following:
  - Great weapon ....4 points
  - Flail ....4 points
  - Spear ....2 points
- May take a shield ....2 points
- May be mounted on one of the following:
  - Skeleton Chariot (See page 91 for profile. Count the cost against your allowance for Heroes. The Tomb Prince replaces the chariot's crew)................55 points
  - Khemrian Warsphinx (See page 93 for points and options. Count the cost against your allowance for Heroes. The Tomb Prince replaces the Warsphinx's crew) ....210 points
- May take magic items up to a total of ....50 points

HEROES

TOMB HERALD — 60 points

Profile	M	WS	BS	S	T	W	I	A	Ld	Troop Type
Tomb Herald	4	4	3	4	4	2	3	3	8	Infantry (Character)

Equipment:
- Hand weapon
- Light armour

Special Rules:
- Flammable
- Killing Blow
- Nehekharan Undead
- Sworn Bodyguard

Options:
- May be armed with one of the following:
  - Great weapon ....4 points
  - Spear ....2 points
  - Halberd...2 points
  - Flail ....4 points
- May take a shield ....2 points
- May be mounted on one of the following:
  - Skeleton Chariot (See page 91 for profile. Count the cost of the chariot against your allowance for Heroes. The Tomb Herald replaces the chariot's crew)............55 points
  - Skeletal Steed..10 points
- May take magic items up to a total of.........................50 points

BATTLE STANDARD BEARER

One Tomb Herald in the army may carry the Battle Standard for +25 points. The Battle Standard Bearer can have a magic standard (no points limit). A model that carries a magic standard cannot have any other magic items.

LICHE PRIEST — 70 points

Profile	M	WS	BS	S	T	W	I	A	Ld	Troop Type
Liche Priest	4	3	3	3	3	2	2	1	7	Infantry (Character)

Magic:
A Liche Priest is a Level 1 Wizard.
He may use spells from one of the following:
- the Lore of Nehekhara
- the Lore of Light
- the Lore of Death.

Equipment:
- Hand weapon

Special Rules:
- Nehekharan Undead

Options:
- May upgrade to a Level 2 Wizard.........35 points
- May be mounted on a Skeletal Steed ......10 points
- May take magic items up to a total of .....50 points

A Liche Priest may be your army's Hierophant, as detailed on page 28.

NECROTECT — 60 points

Profile	M	WS	BS	S	T	W	I	A	Ld	Troop Type
Necrotect	4	3	3	4	4	2	3	2	7	Infantry (Character)

Equipment:
- Hand weapon
- Whip (additional hand weapon)
- Light armour

Special Rules:
- Flammable
- Nehekharan Undead
- Stone Shaper
- Wrath of the Creator
- Hatred

Options:
- May take magic items up to a total of .....50 points

MOUNTS

Profile	M	WS	BS	S	T	W	I	A	Ld	Troop Type
Skeletal Steed	8	2	0	3	3	1	2	1	5	War Beast
Khemrian Warsphinx	6	4	0	5	8	5	1	4	8	Monster
Skeleton Chariot	-	-	-	4	4	3	-	-	-	Chariot (Armour Save 5+)

Special Rules:
- **Skeletal Steed:** Nehekharan Undead.
- **Khemrian Warsphinx:** Animated Construct, Howdah Crew, Large Target, Nehekharan Undead, Terror, Thundercrush Attack.
- **Skeleton Chariot:** 'And the Tomb Kings Rode to War...', Chariot Legions, Nehekharan Undead.

CORE UNITS

SKELETON WARRIORS

4 points per model

Profile	M	WS	BS	S	T	W	I	A	Ld	Troop Type
Skeleton Warrior	4	2	2	3	3	1	2	1	5	Infantry
Master of Arms	4	2	2	3	3	1	2	2	5	Infantry

Unit Size: 10+

Equipment:
- Hand weapon
- Shield

Special Rules:
- Nehekharan Undead

Options:
- May upgrade one Skeleton Warrior to a Master of Arms.................10 points
- May upgrade one Skeleton Warrior to a musician.........................10 points
- May upgrade one Skeleton Warrior to a standard bearer..................10 points
- The entire unit may take any of the following:
  - Spears..1 point per model
  - Light armour...1 point per model

SKELETON ARCHERS

6 points per model

Profile	M	WS	BS	S	T	W	I	A	Ld	Troop Type
Skeleton Warrior	4	2	2	3	3	1	2	1	5	Infantry
Master of Arrows	4	2	3	3	3	1	2	1	5	Infantry

Unit Size: 10+

Equipment:
- Hand weapon
- Bow

Special Rules:
- Arrows of Asaph
- Nehekharan Undead

Options:
- May upgrade one Skeleton Warrior to a Master of Arrows..............10 points
- May upgrade one Skeleton Warrior to a musician.........................10 points
- May upgrade one Skeleton Warrior to a standard bearer..................10 points
- The entire unit may take light armour..............................1 point per model

SKELETON HORSEMEN

12 points per model

Profile	M	WS	BS	S	T	W	I	A	Ld	Troop Type
Skeleton Horseman	4	2	2	3	3	1	2	1	5	Cavalry
Master of Horse	4	2	2	3	3	1	2	2	5	Cavalry
Skeletal Steed	8	2	0	3	3	1	2	1	5	-

Unit Size: 5+

Equipment:
- Hand weapon
- Spear
- Shield

Special Rules:
- Nehekharan Undead
- Vanguard

Options:
- May upgrade one Skeleton Horseman to a Master of Horse.............10 points
- May upgrade one Skeleton Horseman to a musician ....10 points
- May upgrade one Skeleton Horseman to a standard bearer ....10 points
- The entire unit may take light armour............................2 points per model

SKELETON HORSE ARCHERS

14 points per model

Profile	M	WS	BS	S	T	W	I	A	Ld	Troop Type
Skeleton Horseman	4	2	2	3	3	1	2	1	5	Cavalry
Master of Scouts	4	2	3	3	3	1	2	1	5	Cavalry
Skeletal Steed	8	2	0	3	3	1	2	1	5	-

Unit Size: 5+

Equipment:
- Hand weapon
- Bow

Special Rules:
- Arrows of Asaph
- Fast Cavalry
- Nehekharan Undead
- Scouts

Options:
- May upgrade one Skeleton Horseman to a Master of Scouts .... *10 points*
- May upgrade one Skeleton Horseman to a musician .... *10 points*
- May upgrade one Skeleton Horseman to a standard bearer .... *10 points*

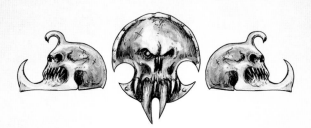

SKELETON CHARIOTS

55 points per model

Profile	M	WS	BS	S	T	W	I	A	Ld	Troop Type
Skeleton Chariot	-	-	-	4	4	3	-	-	-	Chariot (Armour Save 5+)
Skeleton Charioteer	-	3	2	3	-	-	2	2	7	-
Master of Chariots	-	3	2	3	-	-	2	3	7	-
Skeletal Steed	8	2	-	3	-	-	2	1	-	-

Unit Size: 3+

Crew: 2 Skeleton Charioteers

Drawn by: 2 Skeletal Steeds

Equipment (Crew):
- Hand weapon
- Spear
- Bow

Special Rules:
- 'And the Tomb Kings Rode to War…'
- Arrows of Asaph
- Chariot Legions
- Nehekharan Undead

Options:
- One model may upgrade a Charioteer to a Master of Chariots .... *10 points*
- One model may upgrade a Charioteer to a musician .... *10 points*
- One model may upgrade a Charioteer to a standard bearer .... *10 points*
  - One unit's standard bearer may have a magic standard worth up to ... *25 points*

SPECIAL UNITS

TOMB GUARD

11 points per model

Profile	M	WS	BS	S	T	W	I	A	Ld	Troop Type
Tomb Guard	4	3	3	4	4	1	3	1	8	Infantry
Tomb Captain	4	3	3	4	4	1	3	2	8	Infantry

Unit Size: 10+

Equipment:
- Hand weapon
- Light armour
- Shield

Special Rules:
- Killing Blow
- Nehekharan Undead

Options:
- May upgrade one Tomb Guard to a Tomb Captain......................10 points
- May upgrade one Tomb Guard to a musician............................10 points
- May upgrade one Tomb Guard to a standard bearer....................10 points
  - May have a magic standard worth up to............................50 points
- The entire unit may take halberds..............................2 points per model

NECROPOLIS KNIGHTS

65 points per model

Profile	M	WS	BS	S	T	W	I	A	Ld	Troop Type
Necropolis Knight	4	4	3	4	4	1	3	2	8	Monstrous Cavalry
Necropolis Captain	4	4	3	4	4	1	3	3	8	Monstrous Cavalry
Necroserpent	7	3	0	5	4	3	3	3	8	Monstrous Cavalry

Unit Size: 3+

Equipment:
- Spear

Special Rules
- Animated Construct
- Killing Blow (Riders only)
- Nehekharan Undead
- Poisoned Attacks (Necroserpents only)
- Stone Hide

Options:
- May upgrade one Necropolis Knight to a Necropolis Captain...........10 points
- May upgrade one Necropolis Knight to a musician......................10 points
- May upgrade one Necropolis Knight to a standard bearer...............10 points
- May upgrade the entire unit to have the
  Entombed Beneath the Sands special rule.......................5 points per model

TOMB SCORPION

85 points

Profile	M	WS	BS	S	T	W	I	A	Ld	Troop Type
Tomb Scorpion	7	4	0	5	5	3	3	4	8	Monstrous Beast

Unit Size: 1

Special Rules:
- Animated Construct
- Entombed Beneath the Sands
- Killing Blow
- Magic Resistance (1)
- Nehekharan Undead
- Poisoned Attacks

USHABTI

50 points per model

Profile	M	WS	BS	S	T	W	I	A	Ld	Troop Type
Ushabti	5	4	2	4	4	3	3	3	8	Monstrous Infantry
Ushabti Ancient	5	4	2	4	4	3	3	4	8	Monstrous Infantry

Unit Size: 3+

Equipment:
- Hand weapon
- Great weapon

Special Rules:
- Animated Construct
- Arrows of Asaph
- Nehekharan Undead

Options:
- May upgrade one Ushabti to an Ushabti Ancient........................10 points
- May upgrade one Ushabti to a musician................................10 points
- May upgrade one Ushabti to a standard bearer.........................10 points
- The entire unit may replace their great weapons with one of the following:
  - Great bows..free
  - Additional hand weapons...free

SPECIAL UNITS

TOMB SWARM
40 points per base

Profile	M	WS	BS	S	T	W	I	A	Ld	Troop Type
Tomb Swarm	4	3	0	2	2	5	1	5	10	Swarm

Unit Size: 2-10 bases

Special Rules:
- Entombed Beneath the Sands
- Nehekharan Undead
- Poisoned Attacks

CARRION
24 points per model

Profile	M	WS	BS	S	T	W	I	A	Ld	Troop Type
Carrion	2	3	0	4	4	2	3	3	4	War Beast

Unit Size: 3+

Special Rules:
- Fly
- Nehekharan Undead

KHEMRIAN WARSPHINX
210 points

Profile	M	WS	BS	S	T	W	I	A	Ld	Troop Type
Khemrian Warsphinx	6	4	0	5	8	5	1	4	8	Monster
Tomb Guard Crew	-	3	3	4	-	-	3	1	8	

Unit Size:
1 Khemrian Warsphinx
and 4 Tomb Guard crew.

Equipment
(Tomb Guard Crew):
- Spears

Special Rules:
- Animated Construct
- Howdah Crew
- Killing Blow
  (Tomb Guard Crew only)
- Large Target
- Nehekharan Undead
- Terror
- Thundercrush Attack

Options:
- The Khemrian Warsphinx may take any
  of the following:
  - Envenomed Sting...........................*10 points*
  - Fiery Roar....................................*20 points*

SEPULCHRAL STALKERS
55 points per model

Profile	M	WS	BS	S	T	W	I	A	Ld	Troop Type
Sepulchral Stalker	7	3	3	4	4	3	3	2	8	Monstrous Beast

Unit Size: 3+

Equipment:
- Halberd

Special Rules:
- Animated Construct
- Entombed Beneath the Sands
- Nehekharan Undead
- Transmogrifying Gaze

RARE UNITS

NECROLITH COLOSSUS — 170 points

Profile	M	WS	BS	S	T	W	I	A	Ld	Troop Type
Necrolith Colossus	6	3	2	6	6	5	1	4	8	Monster

Unit Size: 1

Equipment:
• Huge sword (hand weapon)

Special Rules
• Animated Construct
• Arrows of Asaph
• Large Target
• Nehekharan Undead
• Terror
• Unstoppable Assault

Options:
• A Necrolith Colossus may be armed with one of the following:
  - Additional hand weapon ....*5 points*
  - Great weapon ....*10 points*
  - Bow of the desert ....*20 points*

HIEROTITAN — 175 points

Profile	M	WS	BS	S	T	W	I	A	Ld	Troop Type
Hierotitan	6	3	0	6	6	5	1	3	8	Monster

Unit Size: 1

Equipment:
• Icon of Ptra
• Scales of Usirian

Special Rules
• Animated Construct
• Large Target
• Nehekharan Undead
• Spirit Conduit
• Terror

NECROSPHINX — 225 points

Profile	M	WS	BS	S	T	W	I	A	Ld	Troop Type
Necrosphinx	6	4	0	5	8	5	1	5	8	Monster

Unit Size: 1

Special Rules:
• Animated Construct
• Decapitating Strike
• Fly
• Killing Blow
• Large Target
• Nehekharan Undead
• Terror

Options:
• A Necrosphinx may take:
  - Envenomed Sting ....*10 points*

SCREAMING SKULL CATAPULT   90 points

Profile	M	WS	BS	S	T	W	I	A	Ld	Troop Type
Screaming Skull Catapult	-	-	-	-	7	3	-	-	-	War Machine (Stone Thrower)
Skeleton Crew	4	2	2	3	3	1	2	1	5	-

Unit Size: 1 Screaming Skull Catapult and 3 Skeleton Crew

Equipment (Crew):
- Hand weapon
- Light armour

Special Rules:
- Nehekharan Undead
- Screaming Skulls

Options:
- May be upgraded to fire Skulls of the Foe.................................*30 points*

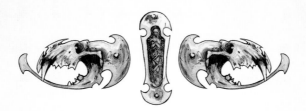

CASKET OF SOULS   135 points

Profile	M	WS	BS	S	T	W	I	A	Ld	Troop Type
Casket of Souls	-	-	-	-	10	3	-	-	-	War Machine
Keeper of the Casket	4	3	3	3	3	1	3	2	8	-
Casket Guard	4	3	3	3	3	1	3	2	8	-

Unit Size: 1 Casket of Souls, 1 Keeper of the Casket and 2 Casket Guard.

Equipment (Crew):
- Great weapons
  (Casket Guard Only)
- Hand weapon (Keeper of the Casket only)
- Light armour

Special Rules
- Covenant of Power
- Killing Blow
  (Casket Guard Only)
- Light of Death
- Nehekharan Undead
- Unleashed Souls

LORDS	M	WS	BS	S	T	W	I	A	Ld	Type	Pg
Arkhan the Black	4	4	3	5	5	3	3	3	9	In(SC)	57
Grand Hierophant Khatep	4	3	3	3	4	3	2	1	9	In(SC)	56
Liche High Priest	4	3	3	3	4	3	2	1	8	In	31
High Queen Khalida	6	6	3	4	5	3	9	5	10	In(SC)	55
Settra the Imperishable	4	7	3	6	5	4	3	5	10	In(SC)	53
- Chariot of the Gods	-	-	-	5	5	5	-	-	-	Ch	
- Skeletal Steed	8	2	-	3	-	-	2	1	-		
Tomb King	4	6	3	5	5	4	3	4	10	In	30

HEROES	M	WS	BS	S	T	W	I	A	Ld	Type	Pg
Liche Priest	4	3	3	3	3	2	2	1	7	In	31
Necrotect	4	3	3	4	4	2	3	2	7	In	33
Prince Apophas	4	4	3	4	3	4	1	5	8	In(SC)	58
Ramhotep the Visionary	4	3	3	4	4	2	3	2	7	In(SC)	59
The Herald Nekaph	4	5	3	4	4	2	3	3	8	In(SC)	54
Tomb Herald	4	4	3	4	4	2	3	3	8	In	32
Tomb Prince	4	5	3	4	5	3	3	3	9	In	30

CORE	M	WS	BS	S	T	W	I	A	Ld	Type	Pg
Skeleton Chariot	-	-	-	4	4	3	-	-	-	Ch	38
- Skeleton Charioteer	-	3	2	3	-	-	2	2	7		
- Master of Chariots	-	3	2	3	-	-	2	3	7		
- Skeletal Steed	8	2	-	3	-	-	2	1	-		
Skeleton Horseman	4	2	2	3	3	1	2	1	5	Ca	36
- Master of Horse	4	2	2	3	3	1	2	2	5		
- Skeletal Steed	8	2	0	3	3	1	2	1	5		
Skeleton Horseman	4	2	2	3	3	1	2	1	5	Ca	37
- Master of Scouts	4	2	3	3	3	1	2	1	5		
- Skeletal Steed	8	2	0	3	3	1	2	1	5		
Skeleton Warrior	4	2	2	3	3	1	2	1	5	In	34
- Master of Arms	4	2	2	3	3	1	2	2	5		
Skeleton Archer	4	2	2	3	3	1	2	1	5	In	35
- Master of Arrows	4	2	3	3	3	1	2	1	5		

SPECIAL	M	WS	BS	S	T	W	I	A	Ld	Type	Pg
Carrion	2	3	0	4	4	2	3	3	4	WB	42
Khemrian Warsphinx	6	4	0	5	8	5	1	4	8	Mo	48
- Tomb Guard Crew	-	3	3	4	-	-	3	1	8		
Necropolis Knight	4	4	3	4	4	1	3	2	8	MC	44
- Necropolis Captain	4	4	3	4	4	1	3	3	8		
- Necroserpent	7	3	0	5	4	3	3	3	8		
Sepulchral Stalker	7	3	3	4	4	3	3	2	8	MB	45
Tomb Guard	4	3	3	4	4	1	3	1	8	In	39
- Tomb Captain	4	3	3	4	4	1	3	2	8		
Tomb Scorpion	7	4	0	5	5	3	3	4	8	MB	47
Tomb Swarm	4	3	0	2	2	5	1	5	10	Sw	43
Ushabti	5	4	2	4	4	3	3	3	8	MI	46
- Ushabti Ancient	5	4	2	4	4	3	3	4	8		

RARE	M	WS	BS	S	T	W	I	A	Ld	Type	Pg
Casket of Souls	-	-	-	-	10	3	-	-	-	WM	40
- Keeper of the Casket	4	3	3	3	3	1	3	2	8		
- Casket Guard	4	3	3	3	3	1	3	2	8		
Hierotitan	6	3	0	6	6	5	1	3	8	Mo	52
Necrolith Colossus	6	3	2	6	6	5	1	4	8	Mo	51
Necrosphinx	6	4	0	5	8	5	1	5	8	Mo	50
Screaming Skull Catapult	-	-	-	-	7	3	-	-	-	WM	41
- Skeleton Crew	4	2	2	3	3	1	2	1	5		

MOUNT	M	WS	BS	S	T	W	I	A	Ld	Type	Pg
Skeletal Steed	8	2	0	3	3	1	2	1	5	WB	Var.
Khemrian Warsphinx	6	4	0	5	8	5	1	4	8	Mo	48
Skeleton Chariot	-	-	-	4	4	3	-	-	-	Ch	38

Troop Type Key: In=*Infantry*, WB=*War Beast*, Ca=*Cavalry*, MI=*Monstrous Infantry*, MB=*Monstrous Beast*, MC=*Monstrous Cavalry*, SC=*Special Character*; Mo=*Monster*, Ch=*Chariot*, Sw=*Swarms*, Un=*Unique*, WM=*War Machine*.